#1 NATIONAL BESTSELLER

Winner of the QWF Mavis Gallant Prize for Non-Fiction

Finalist for the Writers' Trust Shaughnessy
Cohen Prize for Political Writing

Finalist for the B.C. National Award
for Canadian Non-Fiction

Finalist for the J.W. Dafoe Prize

A *Winnipeg Free Press* Top Read of 2014

A *Hill Times* Best Book

An iPolitics Pick "For the Political Junkie"

An Amazon.ca Best Book

"In asking the question no one really wanted to ask two
decades ago—what would have happened if the 'yes' side had
won?—Chantal Hébert has not only sleuthed out the chaos
that would have ensued following the 1995 referendum, she
also trenchantly delineates an enduring warning to all politicians in Canada who might want to change the constitutional
status quo without a coherent, principled strategy. In this clear-
eyed, often gripping account of what was going on in the
minds of the key players, and more ominously, what wasn't
going on, Hébert and her collaborator, Jean Lapierre, have
made a major contribution to our almighty national conun-
drum on what exactly constitutes Canada." BC National Award
for Canadian Non-Fiction jury citation

"It's my job to read Canadian political books (and write the occasional one), but some of the reading this year was more pleasure than work. At the top of my list, *The Morning After*, by my colleague Chantal Hébert (with Jean Lapierre)." Susan Delacourt, Writers' Trust Books of the Year (2014)

"Chantal Hébert . . . [is] one of Canada's best journalists. . . . A gripping story outlining the roles of the major actors in the campaign and the preparations each made for alternative outcomes. Hébert tells the story of a watershed moment in Canadian history and consequent events very well." *The Daily Courier*

"A reader leaves Hébert's and Lapierre's book with the over-whelming impression that with few exceptions—Parizeau, Manning, Chrétien, Romanow—politicians of every stripe managed to bring less thoughtfulness to a campaign over Canada's fate than they do to many more mundane questions." Paul Wells, *Maclean's*

"These co-authors combine their analytical skills and political experience to paint an imaginary and plausible canvas of what-if. Thanks to Hébert's brush, the resulting picture is both believable and revealing, and worth much, much more than a passing look." *Winnipeg Free Press*

CHANTAL HÉBERT

with JEAN LAPIERRE

THE MORNING AFTER

THE 1995 QUEBEC REFERENDUM AND THE DAY THAT ALMOST WAS

LE MATIN SUIVANT

VINTAGE CANADA

Published in Canada by Vintage Canada, a division of
Penguin Random House Canada Limited, in 2015.
Originally published in hardcover in Canada by Alfred A. Knopf Canada,
a division of Penguin Random House Canada Limited, in 2014.
Distributed in Canada by Penguin Random House Canada Limited, Toronto.

Vintage Canada with colophon is a registered trademark.

www.penguinrandomhouse.ca

Library and Archives Canada Cataloguing in Publication

Hébert, Chantal, 1954–, author
The morning after : the 1995 Quebec referendum and the day that almost was /
Chantal Hébert with Jean Lapierre.

Originally published: Toronto: Knopf Canada, 2014.

ISBN 978-0-345-80763-2
eBook ISBN 978-0-345-80764-9

1. Referendum—Québec (Province). 2. Québec (Province)—History—Autonomy
and independence movements. I. Lapierre, Jean, 1956–, author II. Title.

FC2926.9.R4H42 2015   971.4'04   C2014-901251-9

Text and cover design by Andrew Roberts

Image credits: (Jean Chrétien) © Chris Wattie / Reuters,
(Leaders of the Yes side) © Shaun Best / Reuters, both Corbis

Printed and bound in the United States of America

2 4 6 8 9 7 5 3 1

Penguin
Random
House

VINTAGE CANADA

For Clara, Mateo, Alix, Lenox and Mila

CONTENTS

PART 4 **THE PREMIERS**

PART 5 **THE LAST WORD**

A TIMELINE

Nov. 1976   René Lévesque leads the Parti Québécois to power.

May 1980   First Quebec referendum, lost by the sovereignists.

Apr. 1981   The PQ wins a second majority mandate.

Nov. 1981   The first ministers minus Quebec premier René Lévesque
              agree to patriate the Constitution.

Apr. 1982   Patriation of the Constitution by Prime Minister Pierre
              Trudeau.

Sept. 1984   Brian Mulroney's Progressive Conservatives win the federal
              election.

Dec. 1985   Return to power of a federalist government in Quebec
              under Liberal premier Robert Bourassa.

Mar. 1987   The clock runs out on the aboriginal constitutional round.

May 1987   The first ministers unanimously put forward the Meech
              Lake Accord.

Nov. 1988   Brian Mulroney wins a second majority victory.

Sept. 1989   The Quebec Liberals under Robert Bourassa are re-elected
              to a majority government.

June 1990   The clock runs out on the Meech Lake Accord.

Aug. 1992   The first ministers unanimously put forward the
              Charlottetown Accord.

Oct. 1992   The Charlottetown Accord is rejected in a national
              referendum.

June 1993   Kim Campbell beats Jean Charest for the federal Progressive
              Conservative leadership and succeeds Brian Mulroney as
              prime minister.

Oct. 1993	Jean Chrétien leads the federal Liberals to a majority victory. Lucien Bouchard leads the Bloc Québécois to second place and becomes Leader of the Official Opposition. Preston Manning brings fifty-two Reform MPs to the House of Commons.
Mar. 1994	The Action Démocratique du Québec (ADQ) is founded. Mario Dumont steps in as leader a month later.
Sept. 1994	Jacques Parizeau leads the Parti Québécois to a majority government in Quebec.
Dec. 1994	Lucien Bouchard loses a leg to flesh-eating disease.
Oct. 1995	Quebec referendum. Jacques Parizeau resigns.
Jan. 1996	Lucien Bouchard becomes Quebec premier.
June 1997	Jean Chrétien wins a second majority mandate.
Apr. 1998	Jean Charest becomes Quebec Liberal leader.
Nov. 1998	Lucien Bouchard leads the PQ to a second majority mandate.
June 2000	The federal Clarity Act is passed.
Nov. 2000	Jean Chrétien wins a third majority mandate.
Jan. 2001	Lucien Bouchard announces his resignation.
Mar. 2001	Bernard Landry is sworn in as Quebec premier.
Apr. 2003	Jean Charest brings the federalist Quebec Liberals back to government.
Sept. 2012	The Parti Québécois under Pauline Marois returns to power with a minority government.
Apr. 2014	Philippe Couillard leads the Quebec Liberals to a majority government.

Acceptez-vous que le Québec devienne souverain, après avoir offert formellement au Canada un nouveau partenariat économique et politique, dans le cadre du projet de loi sur l'avenir du Québec et de l'entente signée le 12 juin 1995?

Do you agree that Québec should become sovereign, after having made a formal offer to Canada for a new economic and political partnership, within the scope of the Bill respecting the future of Québec and of the agreement signed on June 12, 1995?

OUI
YES

NON
NO

PREFACE

On October 30, 1995, the Canadian federation came within 54,288 votes of having to grapple with the issue of its continued existence. More than four and a half million Quebecers participated in the referendum on Quebec sovereignty that was held that day, and when the votes were counted only a bit more than one percent separated the winners from the losers.

On the morning after, the main protagonists of the duelling campaigns believed that it would not take long—at most a couple of years—before they crossed swords again. The close result suggested that the vote had settled nothing and bore little promise that Quebec and Canada would live happily ever after. And so, expecting they would soon head back to the battle front, the men and women who had led the Yes and No camps were not immediately inclined to lay down their weapons and reflect.

It was the tenth anniversary of the referendum when Radio-Canada produced a documentary titled *Breaking Point* under the direction of veteran journalist Mario Cardinal. He then gathered the material in a book that bears the same name. Pierre Duchesne, a journalist who recently served as a Parti Québécois minister, has done a remarkable job of chronicling Jacques Parizeau's life and times. The last volume of his biographical work deals extensively with the referendum period. For an account of the campaign itself, Cardinal's and Duchesne's works cover the essential territory and more.

But with the twentieth anniversary of the referendum just around the corner, the significance of the day-to-day referendum skirmishes has faded. The October 30 trenches have emptied out. If there were legion halls for constitutional warriors, they would be filled by the retired officers of the 1995 armies. It has taken these men and women two decades, but they are finally ready to reflect on the less than stellar ending to either side's campaign.

When we set out to talk to them in July 2012, there was no referendum in the air. A federalist government was still in power in Quebec and our primary purpose was not to put a spin of one kind or another on the likelihood of yet another referendum. But if we had approached these men and women a year later, at a time when the Parti Québécois was riding high in the polls and a governing majority appeared to be within reach of Premier Pauline Marois, this book might not have seen the light of day. Since then, however, the issue has become moot. In April 2014, Quebecers put the sovereignist dream on indefinite hold. After only eighteen months of Parti Québécois rule, they returned the Liberals to power with a majority government. To all intents and purposes, the election was a referendum on a referendum and the answer was a clear No. That this outcome was achieved in the absence of any promise of constitutional change made its meaning even more devastating for the sovereignist cause.

For this book, Jean Lapierre and I did not ask our host of primarily federal and provincial politicians to refight old battles. Our starting point was the day of the Quebec vote itself and the path we wanted to explore was the one not taken. We wanted to know how they had imagined and prepared for the morning after a federalist defeat.

We did not set out to write the book of revelations or even the book of truth. Two decades have elapsed since the referendum and none of us is the same person that we were on the day after the vote. Our views are inevitably coloured by what has happened since. The eighteen people with whom we spoke were relatively free to embellish their memories or to aggrandize their own roles. Most resisted the temptation valiantly.

The focus of the book is on elected officials or, in the case of former ambassador Raymond Chrétien, on people who held front-line public roles. That is a deliberate choice. Neither of us believes that the pen of history belongs in the hands of unaccountable strategists—as good as they may be at what they do. We did talk to a number of former officials and ex-backroom advisers. They spoke to us on a background basis—usually to fill in some blanks in the narrative of their former political masters. If they read the book they will recognize their contribution. There is one exception. For a long time we were not sure that former premier Jacques Parizeau would relive for us what was for him a more painful day than for anyone else we spoke to. His former chief of staff, Jean

Royer, spoke to us on the record and he is quoted by name in the relevant chapters.

The men and women whose narratives make up the core of this book are retired from politics. Five of them are past Quebec premiers; another four once led their respective provinces. Two are former prime ministers. They hail from every region of the country. Two are from Western Canada, three from Ontario and two from the Atlantic region. Four of the Quebecers fought on the Yes side and one of them— Lucien Bouchard—was a federal politician at the time. The balance is reversed in the case of the Quebecers from the No camp. Six were Members of Parliament in 1995 and only one—Daniel Johnson—sat in the Quebec National Assembly.

For the very last section of the book, we asked the current leaders of the main federal parties to walk us through their own referendum day. We did not want to discuss how they would deal with a future referendum. It was not our objective to anticipate a discussion that remains highly hypothetical. Thomas Mulcair and Justin Trudeau accepted our invitation. Stephen Harper, who was the Reform Party's lead critic on referendum issues in 1995, declined.

Jean Lapierre, a former Member of Parliament, and I conducted most the Quebec interviews together. To a man and a woman, the people we spoke to jointly were more candid in the presence of someone who used to be one of their own than if they had been dealing only with a journalist. It was the persistence of Lapierre that finally unlocked Jacques Parizeau's door. For that we thank the former premier's wife and partner, Lisette Lapointe. With the exception of Sheila

Copps, I talked to the politicians from outside Quebec on my own. And I wrote what you are about to read.

We decided that the best way to illustrate the very different paths that had led us to produce this book was to briefly describe how we had each come to know our eighteen subjects. Since Ottawa and Quebec political junkies will not be able to find the names of their favourite backroom girls and boys in this book, that section is offered to them as a substitute for an index.

We set out on this project like people who embark on a trip to a well-travelled destination; it did not take us long to realize that we were actually on a voyage of discovery. We gained unexpected insights along the way and we shed some illusions. We may be a little bit wiser at the end of this project than when we started out, but what is certain is that we were never bored. We hope you will not be either.

The 1995 referendum has quietly informed the politics of this country for nearly twenty years, but was itself the culmination of a twenty-year constitutional war that consumed the energies of successive prime ministers from Quebec.

It came on the heels of a series of constitutional rounds stretching from the early seventies when the first ministers met in Victoria to the early nineties. Only one of those rounds succeeded. In late 1981 Liberal prime minister Pierre Elliott Trudeau secured the agreement of every premier, with the notable exception of Quebec's René Lévesque, to take control of the Canadian Constitution away from Britain and adopt a Charter of Rights and Freedoms.

Between 1983 and 1987, four first ministers conferences on aboriginal rights took place. The political leaders of the First Nations, the Métis and the Inuit were full participants in the talks, but under the new amending formula they needed the agreement of at least seven premiers representing 50 percent of Canada's population, plus the support of the federal government, to enshrine the right of the country's aboriginal people to self-government in the Constitution. In the end a proposal along lines that met the aspirations of the aboriginal leadership foundered for lack of one province.

Quebec sat as an observer at those aboriginal conferences. Its premiers (PQ and Liberal) abstained from voting in protest over Trudeau's decision to bring the Constitution home without the province's consent. If Quebec had participated fully, the aboriginal amendment would have succeeded. That episode—the first that saw the country's first ministers attempt to effect constitutional change under that amending formula—brought home to Canada's political leadership a new and unsettling reality. For as long as Quebec kept itself out of the constitutional loop, the path to modernizing institutions such as the Senate, enshrining the federation's social union or expanding First Nations' rights would essentially be blocked.

The two subsequent constitutional rounds were held between 1987 and 1992 and they resulted in two separate series of draft amendments designed to normalize Quebec's participation in the constitutional process.

The first—agreed to unanimously at Meech Lake— would have seen Quebec's status as a "distinct society" enshrined in the Constitution. It prevented future federal governments from launching programs in areas such as education or health that fell under the constitutional authority of the provinces without their consent. It handed Quebec control over the immigration on its territory. Also, the accord gave the provinces a say in future Senate appointments and guaranteed that three of the nine seats on the Supreme Court would continue to be held by Quebec justices—trained in the province's civil law system.

Finally it granted Quebec a veto on future changes to the Constitution.

The second accord—finalized in August 1992 in Charlottetown and also agreed to unanimously by all first ministers—touched on just about every aspect of constitutional change, from Quebec's distinctive place in the federation to Senate reform and aboriginal rights. Both foundered, exacerbating tensions between Quebec and the rest of Canada in the process and exposing a deep rift between the country's political elites and the electorate.

Across three decades marked by constitutional warfare, the scenario of a possible break-up of the federation was never completely off Canada's political radar; it might never be. From 1976 onward, champions of the Quebec sovereignty movement were either direct participants in the constitutional negotiations or else keeping watch on the proceedings from the official opposition benches of the National Assembly.

At the initiative of the Parti Québécois in 1980, the question of whether Quebecers wanted to leave the Canadian federation was asked and answered in the negative by a proportion of 60 percent. By the time of the last failed attempt at constitutional reconciliation with Quebec, in 1992, a sovereignist party—the Bloc Québécois—had appeared in the House of Commons.

Between 1980 and 1995 the sovereignty movement had expanded its parliamentary presence from Quebec City to Ottawa and its case for separation was bolstered by successive constitutional crises. In September 1995, the Parti Québécois introduced Bill 1: An Act Respecting the Future of Quebec. If sovereignty prevailed in that fall's referendum, the bill would authorize the National Assembly to proclaim the province's independence from Canada within a year. The possibility that Quebecers could opt to separate was never more real than in the dying hours of the 1995 referendum. With polls showing the sovereignist Yes campaign in the lead during the last week before Quebecers decided their political fate, the politicians who manned the front lines in Quebec and across Canada were forced to look down in the so-called dark hole of a pro-secession vote and prepare for the possible morning after a federalist defeat in Quebec.

These are some of their stories.

PART 1

THE YES CAMP

CHAPTER 1

THE PAPER TIGER: LUCIEN BOUCHARD

Few people can claim to have single-handedly changed the course of history. On the morning of October 30, 1995, Lucien Bouchard believed he was about to do just that. "I was never one to use the word *historic* in my speeches. In politics, it is a term that is too often abused. But on that morning, I told myself that it was probably going to be a historic day in the true sense of the word. Quebec was about to fully take its place in history."

The pollsters who had been tracking the vote for the pro-sovereignty side as referendum day approached were as categorical as they could be. The lead that the Yes camp had built since mid-campaign had held over the final weekend before the Monday vote. As long as the well-oiled sovereignist machine got the vote out, the Yes camp would have a rendezvous with history that very night.

The hard-nosed strategists who ran the campaign concurred. Many of them had memories of the beating their side had taken in the 1980 referendum. They had lost that vote by twenty points. Fifteen years later, the end of this second campaign had a very different feel.

In twenty-five years, no sovereignist party had ever managed to cross the 50 percent line in a federal, provincial or referendum vote. But the leaders of Quebec's sovereignty movement were convinced that the referendum results would make up for a quarter of a century of near misses. For the first time ever a majority of Quebecers would line up behind the sovereignist option.

So confident was the Bloc Québécois leader that he prepared only one speech for that night's Yes rally. It was a victory address. "People think that politicians always write two speeches but on that occasion I wrote only one, the real one," he recalls about the undelivered draft that he wrote out in longhand.

If his side prevailed, Bouchard expected the result to pave the way to the tough negotiation of a different relationship between Quebec and the Canadian federation. On the morning of the referendum, that upcoming battle was naturally on his mind. But so was another battle of wills that was already playing out on a different front.

Before a single vote was cast or counted, a power struggle for control of the post-victory agenda was underway among the partners who made up the pro-sovereignty coalition. The façade of unity cemented by short-term electoral necessity was showing cracks.

Bouchard—whom so many Quebecers expected to see at centre ice in the aftermath of a Yes victory—felt that he was being forced out of the play. "Jacques Parizeau's people were even more convinced than I was that we were about to win. In their minds, it was a done deal. I sensed that all the compromises that had been arrived at to give me more space in the campaign were behind them. The message was that the premier was back in charge."

The star of the Yes camp sensed that he was fast exhausting his usefulness to the man under whose orders he was expected to lead Quebecers to independence. With the campaign barely over, Bouchard's role was about to be downgraded from indispensable to disposable. He was determined not to let that happen.

Almost twenty years after the fact, the Parizeau and Bouchard teams still cannot agree how things played out between them over the course of that fateful day. To listen to the former Bloc Québécois leader, he was systematically given the cold shoulder. His calls to Parizeau went unreturned and his queries ignored. "I could not talk with Mr. Parizeau or with people close to him. I simply could not get through to them."

Mario Dumont—the leader of the Action Démocratique party (ADQ) and third partner in the Yes triumvirate—and Bob Dufour—Bouchard's long-time political organizer—both back the latter's recollection of events. But Parizeau's right-hand man, Jean Royer, offers a contrary view. The premier's former chief of staff says he personally took care to liaise with Bouchard and his entourage throughout the day.

What remains uncontested is that between the time the polls opened that Monday morning and until defeat was certain late that night, the federal leader of the opposition and the premier never exchanged a word—not to coordinate an evening that both believed would be momentous for

Quebec and certainly not to discuss their plan for the critical hours after a Yes vote.

In politics, nights on which every word counts are few and far between. Yet Parizeau and Bouchard did not so much as compare notes ahead of the referendum-night rally. With the eyes of the world riveted on them and on the province they sought to lead to nationhood, they never discussed what spin they would give to a result that was expected to be historic but also fairly close. "Until early in the evening, we had no sense from the Parizeau people how events would unfold after the Yes had won. The premier was incommunicado." At some point over the course of the day, Parizeau taped a victory speech for television. Bouchard says he had no direct input in that speech: "He taped his grand address without telling us." Had the two leaders discussed any of this, they might have found themselves on different pages.

That Monday evening, Bouchard and Parizeau watched from different suites of the Montreal Palais des congrès as the referendum results came in; but it wasn't until minutes before Bouchard delivered an improvised concession speech that they finally spoke, and even then only by cellphone as the Bloc leader was making his way to the stage.

Bouchard says that he laid out for the premier what he was going to say: he would concede defeat and planned to use his speech to start the healing process.

The issue of its political future had just split Quebec wide open: 50.6 percent had voted no and 49.4 percent had voted yes. Fewer than 55,000 out of almost 5 million votes separated the winners from the losers.

Bouchard recalls Parizeau saying that his own speech would be quite different.

No one, including Bouchard himself, remembers much of what he said that night. "I was making it up as I went along since I had no prepared notes. It was anything but a great speech. I was just going through the motions. Everyone in the room was heartbroken and no one really liked my speech. I could sense as much. I concluded by saying that we should not lose hope; that the next time would be the right one."

Even if Bouchard had wanted to give a speech for the history books, he would have been wasting his breath. With bitter words that blamed "money" and some "ethnic votes" for the narrow defeat, Parizeau—for once in the referendum saga—stole the show from his Bloc partner.

By the time the premier began his speech, Bouchard and Mario Dumont had vanished from sight. Unsure what the premier was going to say but sensing that he was in a deep funk, they decided to leave the stage and avoid one last show of strained solidarity.

In hindsight, Bouchard and Dumont both feel they dodged a bullet that night. Their absence made the task of distancing themselves from the premier's controversial remarks easier. "After that speech I did not want to talk to anybody," says Bouchard. He, his wife, Audrey Best, and his entourage left the convention centre by the back door and through the underground parking.

The heartbreaking result of the referendum had drained Bouchard. The adrenaline that had sustained him over the course of the campaign was gone. By referendum night, he had been living on that adrenaline for seven years. For political and personal reasons, they had been the most intense years of his life to date.

Between the spring of 1988, when he relinquished the post of Canada's ambassador to France to enter politics at the invitation of Prime Minister Brian Mulroney, and the night of October 30, 1995, Bouchard had been campaigning continuously. And until that evening, he had been on a non-stop winning streak.

By June 1988, Bouchard had been in politics for only a few months when he successfully ran for a federal seat as a Progressive Conservative in a by-election held in his native Lac-Saint-Jean. With a general election looming, his primary mission was to restore the tarnished ethical image of Mulroney's Quebec caucus.

A few months later Bouchard was playing a leading role in the federal election dominated by the issue of free trade. Without Quebec, Mulroney could not win a second majority mandate and his free trade initiative would be stillborn. Bouchard had a big hand in the 1988 Tory victory.

Eighteen months later, the star recruit had burned the bridges that that election had built him. At the time of his swearing-in to the federal cabinet, Bouchard had said that he had been drawn into the political arena by Mulroney's constitutional efforts and the still-to-be-ratified Meech Lake Accord, which the prime minister had successfully negotiated with the premiers in 1987. But in the spring of 1990—with the window to ratify the accord set to close—the prime minister was still scrambling to accommodate the three provinces that had yet to come on board. Those efforts did not sit well with Bouchard. In late May he resigned to sit as an independent in protest over what he feared would be the inevitable dilution of the Quebec-focused agreement and, in particular, its distinct society clause. A bit more than a month later, the Meech Lake Accord was consigned to the history books as Canada's most divisive constitutional failure.

In the weeks after the dismal end of that saga, Bouchard recruited Gilles Duceppe—a trade union negotiator and the son of a much loved, much respected actor—to run for a Montreal seat under the new banner of what would a year later officially become the Bloc Québécois. Against the backdrop of the Meech failure, Duceppe won the inner city riding Laurier–Sainte-Marie, a traditionally Liberal seat, with 70 percent of the vote.

Two years later Bouchard took on his former Tory colleagues in a national referendum on the Charlottetown Accord. That constitutional deal was meant to be a substitute for the failed Meech initiative. In October 1992 it was rejected by a slim majority of Canadians that included a slightly larger majority of Quebecers.

In 1993, he led his newly created Bloc Québécois into its first election campaign, winning fifty-four of seventy-five Quebec seats and the title of official opposition in the House of Commons. A year later, he had campaigned hard for the provincial Parti Québécois and helped Parizeau bring sovereignists back to government in Quebec City after an absence of a decade from the corridors of power.

Over the same intense political period, Lucien Bouchard remarried and became a father—twice. Just one year before the referendum campaign, he almost lost his life to flesh-eating disease, an episode that cost him a leg but would elevate his status to political sainthood in Quebec.

As they considered the close results of the referendum late the night of October 30, most pundits and many politicians predicted a quick rematch and that the odds would likely favour a different outcome. Bouchard did not agree. "I could not see another referendum taking place quickly. I felt that there was a lot of fatigue, that we had given it all that we could and that we had exhausted ourselves. We were missing only an inch but that was all the ground that there was to be had. I could not see us doing it again anytime soon."

Part of the fatigue was very much his own: "I had the feeling of having done all that I had done, all that I had sacrificed, including part of my health, for nothing. I felt I had fallen from the peak of hope to the abyss of discouragement."

He and Audrey Best agreed that he was done with politics. "We decided I would wrap up the session in Ottawa and then return to a law practice in Montreal. I had cut myself off from my professional environment when I had founded the Bloc. I could not count on a lot of help. But we did not have a rich lifestyle. We had small kids. We were used to tightening our belts."

Bouchard's descent into gloom did not last long. Less than twenty-four hours later, Jacques Parizeau resigned and the

Bloc Québécois leader was offered the premier's job on a plat-
ter, an offer he subsequently accepted. But Bouchard never
did get to see if he could advance the extra inch that separated
him from his goal on the night of October 30, 1995.

History can never know exactly how many of the Quebecers
who voted yes in 1995 dared to do so only because Lucien
Bouchard assured them he had their backs. There is plenty of
anecdotal and polling evidence that suggests that number
was high.

In the dying weeks of the campaign, his sudden appearance on centre stage as the future chief negotiator of a
sovereignty-seeking Quebec reversed the tide of public
opinion in favour of the Yes camp. Until then, over the
period that Bouchard spent in the background, support for
the sovereignist side in the polls remained mired in the
low forties.

Every single person interviewed for this book has
described the replacement of Premier Jacques Parizeau by
Lucien Bouchard as the lead campaigner for the Yes camp as
a game-changer. No one really saw it coming, in large part
because it went against the very grain of conventional political campaigning.

There was no Canadian precedent for a mid-campaign
correction of the scope the Yes side underwent during the
referendum and no reason to believe they could pull it off. On
paper, replacing one lead campaigner with another overnight

looked like a prescription for disaster. It would have been construed as desperation, making the team that had to go to such extremes come across as a collection of amateurs. Except that in this instance it worked so well that it shattered the best laid plans of federalist strategists on Parliament Hill and on the ground in Quebec.

A formidable public speaker with charisma to boot, Bouchard enjoyed a unique connection with Quebec voters. For many non-Quebecers, Bouchard's resignation from Brian Mulroney's Progressive Conservative cabinet over the Meech Lake failure was an act of betrayal perpetrated against a man who was not only the prime minister but also a personal friend and a political benefactor. But in Quebec, Bouchard was widely seen as a man of principle, ready to put his career and his health on the line for a cause and for his people. The makeover operation placed Bouchard squarely and solely in the window—and relegated Premier Parizeau whose appeal was essentially limited to ardent sovereignist believers—to second-tier venues, a kind of B-circuit designed to avoid distracting the media from the main event.

It worked like magic.

In less than a week, confidence changed sides. With it, momentum—the essential ingredient of all electoral victories—switched to the Yes camp.

A week before the referendum, polls showed that the pro-sovereignty option enjoyed a solid lead in voting intentions, and the federalist brain trust was scrambling for an effective response. In some polls, support for the Yes rose as high as 56 percent.

With Bouchard in the driver's seat, a critical number of apprehensive voters resolved to make the leap of faith required to jump on the sovereignty bandwagon. For many, his presence on the front line acted as a psychological safety net. They trusted that throughout the secession process he would place their best interests above all else—especially if it came to negotiating full-fledged independence for the province. They trusted his intentions and they trusted his negotiating skills.

As tactics go, it was a stroke of genius. In substance, it bordered on misleading advertising.

What voters did not know as they headed to the polls in droves was that they were about to entrust their political future to a paper tiger. Bouchard might have looked like the commanding figure on the sovereignist chessboard but ultimately he was just the biggest pawn in Parizeau's great game. His strategic value was programmed to decline from the moment that the polling stations opened and all was in place to confine his post-referendum moves to a corner of the board. His title of chief negotiator was essentially an impromptu label designed to enhance his gravitas as he sought Quebecers' support for sovereignty. It was not backed by a contract—moral or otherwise—with Parizeau and his team.

"There never was a discussion as to my mandate. It happened very quickly, in quasi-desperate circumstances, over a matter of hours. I was told [second-hand by a Parizeau emissary] that I was negotiator-in-chief and we used the title to get votes. I certainly did not get a five-year contract," quips Bouchard about his elevation to the front line.

He might have been out of the spotlight, but the premier was and remained the de facto leader of the Yes camp.

Bouchard says he was not aware of the specifics of the preparations Parizeau had undertaken to get Quebec through the immediate aftermath of a Yes vote. He didn't know that the premier already had a plan to prevent, or at least blunt, a whiplash on the financial markets, nor that committees had been tentatively assembled to lay the groundwork for post-victory negotiations with Canada.

"I knew absolutely nothing about any of that," says Bouchard. "I was on the bus, delivering three or four speeches a day. We were not sleeping. We just kept going. I was not at all prepared for the role of lead campaigner. The initial plan had been that I would focus on question period on Parliament Hill with some travel on the side. We had developed no themes, no speeches. I entered into it without any preparation."

Nor was he a part of all of the exploratory discussions Parizeau's emissaries had held with people close to federal politicians such as Reform Party leader Preston Manning or to some of the feelers the premier had sent out to various international figures. "There was simply no time for anything except making speech after speech after speech."

The logistical difficulties attendant on bringing Parizeau and Bouchard together in the heat of a campaign were only part of the reason why there was no serious effort to sketch out Bouchard's post-referendum role and put meat on the bone of his lofty, confidence-inspiring title. If the premier and the Bloc leader had sat down to discuss the way forward, differences that could hardly be resolved as the campaign raged on would inevitably have surfaced. It had been obvious for some time that they did not see eye to eye on strategy before the referendum, and some of those differences endured to the day of the vote.

Parizeau had initially planned to go into the referendum with a harder question, one that would not have involved a future association with Canada. What the premier had in mind was a divorce, pure and simple, possibly, but not necessarily, on amicable terms.

If given a Yes vote, he did not believe that Canada would cut off its nose to spite its face. It could not prevent a sovereign Quebec from continuing to use the Canadian dollar as its currency (although it could refuse the former province a say on monetary policy). Parizeau was also convinced that Canada would not blockade an independent Quebec because that would mean cutting itself off from the Atlantic provinces.

The Canadian federation minus Quebec would be dominated by Ontario—a next-door neighbour whose economy was then more closely linked to Quebec than to Western Canada. The Quebec/Ontario trade routes to the U.S. routinely crossed into each other's territory. And Parizeau believed that, in the end, no federal government would risk putting one-year-old NAFTA—the free trade agreement that linked Canada, the United States and Mexico—in peril by demanding that Quebec be written out of it. If one did,

Parizeau calculated that the United States would push for a quick resolution to minimize trade disruptions. He thought he could make a good case that a sovereign Quebec should be grandfathered into NAFTA without the agreement having to be renegotiated.

But Lucien Bouchard would not seek a divorce without tagging a joint custody agreement onto Parizeau's terms. The Bloc Québécois leader was convinced that the quality of the post-Yes relationship between Quebec and Canada would loom large in the minds of voters when they cast their ballots in the referendum. He personally believed that the preferred economic relationship currently enjoyed by Quebec and the rest of Canada was mutually beneficial and that it should be maintained. He thought that common political institutions such as a European Union–style parliament should be crafted to oversee that relationship.

Bouchard had forced the premier's hand on the issue by calling—in public—for an addition to the referendum question: an offer of an economic and political partnership to be made to Canada after a Yes vote. To increase the Yes camp's appeal to voters, he had also brought Mario Dumont and his soft-nationalist ADQ party under the tent. He expected Dumont to be a key ally in his own post-victory dealings with Parizeau.

That conflict had played out during the spring leading up to the campaign and it had rocked the unity of the sovereignist camp. Parizeau had been forced to relent, but in his book a Yes vote remained a green light to make Quebec a sovereign country, whether he had a partnership with Canada or not. What was less well known was Bouchard's deeply held conviction that there should and would be a second referendum to confirm Quebecers' support for a different relationship with Canada before the province's new status materialized.

He had made the case for a ratification referendum to Parizeau face to face shortly before the October referendum campaign began. Each leader had brought only one aide to that meeting and Mario Dumont was not invited. "I told Parizeau: we will go seek a mandate to negotiate [a partnership] but we will also tell Quebecers that we will come back to ask them to pronounce on the result. On that basis, we will win a solid enough mandate to wrestle something acceptable at the negotiating table."

To this day, Bouchard remains convinced that his two-step proposal was "the sensible option" and a winning approach. He feels that, under those conditions, he would have won the 1995 referendum with 55 percent of the vote. "With that plan, we could have obtained a real mandate because Quebecers would have known that they would have the last word. The Quebec people would not have put themselves in the hands of two or three guys who would ultimately decide on its behalf."

Parizeau had rejected the idea of a second referendum. He feared a repeat of the 1980 episode, when 60 percent of Quebecers had refused René Lévesque's first PQ government a mandate to negotiate sovereignty-association because the prospects for a future association seemed uncertain.

Even more fundamentally, he felt that there should be minimal links between a sovereign Quebec and Canada. He was wary of any arrangement that smacked of substantial integration. He was determined not to go through the battle to win a mandate for sovereignty only to end up with renewed federalism. In the eyes of the premier, Bouchard's partnership could easily become a step down the slippery slope to re-confederation rather than full nationhood.

Bouchard was of the opposite persuasion. He fully expected the Canadian authorities to demand a repeat vote.

"I could not imagine that they would say, yes, you are sovereign. We accept your sovereignty. They would have asked for another referendum. I know that Mr. Parizeau would not have wanted that. He would have preferred to declare independence unilaterally. But I thought we might need to do a second one and that if we worked hard at the negotiating table, we could get ourselves an even stronger mandate."

Given those differences, reciprocal suspicion dominated the two men's relationship. In the event of a victory, there would be precious little trust between the chief negotiator and the premier, and the latter was determined to call the shots.

Parizeau and Bouchard were both aware that their alliance was a marriage of convenience—designed to last as long as the campaign required but not necessarily much longer or, at least, not without some reckoning of the significant gap between their takes on the follow-up to a referendum victory.

In the months and years after the 1995 referendum defeat, Bouchard came to the conclusion that Parizeau's endorsement of his role as negotiator-in-chief was strictly opportunistic. He says he learned only after the fact about some of the studies on post-referendum issues that Parizeau had commissioned. Further, he was not consulted about who else would be on the team that the premier had begun to assemble for the post-Yes negotiations. "It's normal to set up such a committee. But I can't help wondering what would have happened to me if I had suddenly been thrown into the mix. Was there really a role for me in the operation?"

In June 1995, only a few months before the referendum campaign was scheduled to get underway, Parizeau had travelled to Ottawa for a private reception with the ambassadors to Canada of the European Union countries. A few of them had asked what would happen if, having said yes to his referendum question in the fall, Quebecers subsequently changed their minds before the premier had had a chance to proclaim the province's independence or to have it recognized by the international community.

Parizeau had answered that it would be too late to reverse course. For Quebecers to vote yes in the referendum would be akin to a lobster swimming into a trap, he told his hosts for the sake of illustrating his point. There would be no way to back out of it.

On the day of the referendum, with victory that night very much on his mind, Bouchard was already swimming hard to avoid becoming Parizeau's biggest catch.

In his wildest dreams, Bouchard did not expect his side to win the referendum by a large margin. "No one thought we would get to 55 percent or 60 percent. But anything over 50 percent would have been a big victory for Quebec sovereignty. No sovereignist party had ever managed to win more than 50 percent of the vote in any general election."

But despite that bullish assessment, it is far from clear that he believed a referendum victory would lead to an independent Quebec. After a Yes vote secured by the narrowest of margins, Bouchard was convinced that Canada would eventually agree to sit down and talk, albeit not necessarily to set Quebec's departure from the federation in motion. "It is clear that a 51 percent mandate is not as strong as a 60 percent one but it is a mandate, and I thought that if the federal government did not play nice, if it refused to sit down and talk, if it was contemptuous of the result, we would go back to the people and get a 60 percent mandate out of the backlash that would have resulted from the Canadian attitude.

"They [the rest of Canada's political elite] would have figured it out. They were politicians and they were wise. Some were very respectful of democracy. They would have thought it through and said: let's strike a deal. But what that deal would have been, I don't know except that it would certainly be better than what we have now."

He is certain that if Canada had taken a hard line on the referendum result, if its political leadership had refused to sit down and talk with the Yes camp, Parizeau would have quickly and unilaterally declared Quebec's independence. He notes that, in the event of an early impasse with Canada, the premier had already made his intentions clear to Quebecers.

Bill 1, the draft bill on sovereignty that laid out the post-Yes roadmap, declared that the time frame to arrive at a partnership with the rest of Canada would not be open-ended, that if negotiations failed sovereignty would be declared unilaterally.

"Even I could not have stopped him. No one could have stopped Parizeau. And he would have been justified in doing it. It is not true that faced with a federal refusal to acknowledge the referendum decision, Quebecers would have said: fine, we will just forget about it. It would not have happened this way."

In Bouchard's mind, and in spite of the year's time that Parizeau had conceded to transition to Quebec's independence, a federal refusal to accept the result could have triggered an immediate unilateral declaration of independence (UDI), as quickly as "within twenty-four hours," he suggests. "As of the moment that you can unilaterally declare your independence because you have invited the other side to talk and it has refused, even Canada's foreign allies would have had to acknowledge the stalemate."

But had Canada sat down to talk, Bouchard, chief negotiator with a fragile mandate, sounds today as if he could have considered something less than sovereignty as the outcome of negotiations with Canada.

Two decades later, he will go no further than to assert that there would have been a deal of some sort. "I am convinced that we would have changed things but to what degree? The answer to that question is not obvious but there would have been changes. It would have been an enormous gain on the scale of the status quo and certainly a lot better than whatever René Lévesque achieved in 1981 when he went to negotiate constitutional change on his knees," he says. "You can send your best and brightest to negotiate on your behalf—and we did—but they will always lose if they don't have a mandate to back them up."

In his dreams here is what he thought his opening gambit to Canada's representatives would be: "You have in front of you a guy called Lucien Bouchard. He is not a bad guy but he is no Einstein. But he is elected and, more importantly, he is not there on his own behalf but on that of the Quebec people who, in a proportion of 51 percent, have given him a mandate to come to you. It is they who are speaking. In negotiation, that is a strong statement. Without a mandate, one goes nowhere."

Bouchard knew what opening statement he wanted to make to Canada's negotiators, but he did not know who those negotiators would be. "No one on the federal side had a mandate to negotiate Quebec's sovereignty. What we would initially have done would have been to issue an invitation to the federal authorities and maybe to the provinces to meet us in short order."

In one scenario he imagined Jean Chrétien sitting across the table from him, albeit alongside a string of non-Quebec federal politicians. "They [other Canadians] would have wanted to surround him with many of their own." In another, he speculates that the provinces would have stepped up to the plate and insisted on being at the table alongside the federal government.

He says he can't imagine Ontario, for one, not claiming a seat for itself at the negotiations. A scenario that would have involved the full participation of the provinces is the one he says he would have preferred because "I was friends with the premiers, really friends with all of them."

But that view benefits from a significant dose of hindsight. Over his time as premier, Bouchard did strike up friendships with many of his provincial peers—notably Ontario's Mike Harris, Manitoba's Gary Filmon, Saskatchewan's Roy Romanow and Newfoundland's Brian Tobin. All of them speak well of him and of their time together around the provincial table. But those friendships came about some time after the 1995 referendum. On the actual morning after the vote, Bouchard had no personal rapport with most of the men who would soon be his fellow premiers. And he very much was the number-one enemy of Canada's political class, including the premiers.

It has been said in the years that have elapsed since the referendum that Bouchard was secretly relieved to lose by a narrow margin rather than win with the smallest of leads. But he rejects the notion when it is put to him. "That is completely crazy. I would have taken any win and run with it and we would have gotten some progress out of it. I believe that if we had won the referendum, we would have secured something extraordinarily good for Quebec."

And what of Parizeau in all this? As of the morning after a referendum victory, Bouchard was well aware that the ball would be back in the premier's court. In practical terms, his Quebec partner would have the upper hand. "As premier, he had the power. He was the one who could present and pass legislation. He had a government and the legitimacy that comes with it. He could have terminated my services as chief negotiator."

But in the same breath, Bouchard notes that it might not have been easy for Parizeau to cast aside an ally who happened to be the Leader of the Official Opposition in Ottawa (not to mention the most popular political figure in Quebec). And while he maintains that the two would "have been condemned to come to work together," he is careful not to say on whose terms that would have happened.

In fact, in the days leading up to the referendum, Bouchard had started to prepare for an inevitable showdown with Parizeau. As Quebecers went to the polls to cast their ballot, the two leading figures of the Yes camp were already headed for what stood to become a fight to a knockout finish. Their shadowboxing on referendum day was just the warm-up act.

CHAPTER 2

THE RELUCTANT SOVEREIGNIST: MARIO DUMONT

H ad Quebecers voted yes, neither Jacques Parizeau—the lifelong sovereignist warrior—nor Lucien Bouchard—the charismatic future negotiator-in-chief—would have been the first leader of the winning coalition taking to the podium to map out the road ahead. That honour would have fallen to the twenty-something leader of a party so green that he was its one and only MNA.

On the day of the referendum, Mario Dumont had barely celebrated the first anniversary of his entry into the National Assembly. His party, the Action Démocratique du Québec, had been on the Quebec map for less than two years. Of the three leaders who made up the sovereignist coalition, the youthful Dumont was the only one who could have been mistaken for a prototype of a younger generation of progressive pro-sovereignty Quebecers. In fact, he was anything but that. A fiscal conservative whose moderate approach to nationalism had initially leaned toward a reform of federalism rather than outright independence, Dumont was typical of the soft nationalists whose support was so essential to the

Yes camp. It was with that constituency in mind that the offer of partnership between a sovereign Quebec and Canada was tagged onto the referendum question.

On an evening of such historic importance, to be first in line to the podium is to occupy a strategic position. In the event of a Yes win, and with the world watching, Dumont, Bouchard and Parizeau were in place to immediately set the tone for the sovereignist offensive. Dumont would address an overheated crowd largely made up of sovereignist believers who had been waiting decades for such a night. They would need no warm-up act. But his purpose was strikingly different. He was on a mission to cool heads.

The ADQ leader was determined to use—in light of his party's modest representation in the National Assembly—what stood to be his last fifteen minutes in the spotlight for a while to slow down the momentum of a sovereignist victory. "If the result had been a narrow Yes, my speech would have been a prudent one. I would have spoken of a victory, but I would also have left myself a number of doors open to prevent Parizeau from racing off with the result like a wild horse."

That intention put Dumont on a straight collision course with the premier and the Parti Québécois brain trust. Parizeau's referendum night strategy called for doing as much as he could to give the result an aura of irreversibility. That goal had been top of mind when he had pre-taped a television address earlier in the afternoon, just as all the first post-referendum moves his government had in store were designed to achieve that effect.

Despite his many preparations, Parizeau spent surprisingly little time ensuring that no light could shine between his victory-speech spin and that of his ADQ ally. Parizeau might not have been aware of Dumont's mindset, but Bouchard had to have been. And Dumont for one was convinced that he had the Bloc Québécois' blessing to step on the brake.

Dumont had come late to the Yes coalition, in late spring 1995, and largely at Bouchard's pressing invitation. For the ADQ, the proposed Quebec/Canada partnership was the main attraction.

On paper, the ADQ—with its sole MNA—might not have looked like a prize catch for the Yes camp. It was not as if the sovereignty movement lacked for support in Quebec's civil society. Its allies included most of the big union leaders, a strong majority of the province's social activists as well as scores of artists and intellectuals.

But Dumont served an essential purpose. With the young leader onside, Bouchard had belatedly forced Parizeau to put the post-referendum partnership with Canada in the picture. And the presence of a reluctant sovereignist such as Dumont in the lineup gave much-needed gravitas to that late addition.

In the internal dynamics of the Yes camp, Dumont's arrival also helped to balance the scales of power, which had so far given Parizeau—a sitting premier with a government at his command—a de facto edge over Bouchard, who was mere opposition leader in a hostile federal Parliament.

But Dumont never made a secret of the fact that he was driven by fundamentally different motivations than Parizeau and the Parti Québécois. "The difference between me and Parizeau is that it was not that important for me to see a Quebec flag at the United Nations. I believed that, at that particular juncture, the best choice for Quebec was to vote yes. I sincerely believed that voting no amounted to weakening Quebec's hand. But I had not given and did not want to give my life to the cause of sovereignty. It was not my ultimate goal."

The sheer fact that Dumont was on the Yes stage at all on the night of the referendum was a token of the extraordinary events that conspired to give the sovereignist movement this second shot at winning over a majority of Quebecers. On the heels of René Lévesque's 1980 referendum defeat, many observers thought that Quebecers had bolted the door shut to secession. Few sovereignists—even in diehard quarters of the movement—had dared dream that another propitious opportunity would materialize fifteen years later. It was not an opportunity of their own making; the circumstances that led Quebecers like Dumont into the Yes camp were essentially made in Canada.

Unlike many of his francophone contemporaries, Dumont had the natural political instincts of a federalist. He joined the Quebec Liberal Party as a teen and found himself on the fast track in very short order. More than a few Liberals—including then-premier Robert Bourassa, who saw Dumont as a bit of a spiritual son—believed that he would grow up to one day lead the party and eventually the province.

By the time the Meech Lake constitutional crisis came about in 1990, Dumont was the president of the Liberal youth wing and one of the party's rising stars. For him as for scores of like-minded Quebecers, the failure of the accord had proven to be a watershed moment.

In 1982, Quebec—through the voice of its sovereignist government—had refused to join the federal government and the nine other provinces in support of the patriation of the Constitution and the introduction of a Charter of Rights and Freedoms. The return to power in Quebec of a Bourassa-led federalist government three years later had prompted a new round of negotiations designed to formally bring the province back into the constitutional fold. The Meech Lake Accord was the product of that round.

The package met with the immediate and overwhelming approval of Quebec voters, and that support was sustained over the three years that elapsed between its initial 1987 negotiation and a mid-1990 final deadline for its ratification. The PQ, however, never liked the accord negotiated at Meech Lake and argued that it was not good enough. Still a significant majority of Quebecers—more than 60 percent—begged to differ.

The accord did not fare so well in the rest of Canada. Very early on former prime minister Pierre Elliott Trudeau had taken issue with the deal, describing it as an ominous development for the federation that would emasculate its central government. Trudeau intensely disliked the distinct society clause. He opposed the limits on federal spending power. He accused his successor, Brian Mulroney, of having sold out crucial federal powers to the provinces, in particular to the Quebec government, to get a deal.

Trudeau's constitutional perspective was at odds with mainstream Quebec public opinion and with the province's chattering class. His stance may actually have consolidated support for it.

But outside Quebec, over the three years of the accord's existence, support for it steadily declined. In many quarters, initial indifference gave way to open hostility. On June 23, 1990, the deadline for its ratification came and went. The federal government had failed to obtain the signatures of Manitoba and Newfoundland and the accord was formally consigned to the political grave.

In the wake of Meech Lake's demise, Dumont was among the Liberals who called on Premier Bourassa to adopt a more aggressive constitutional stance. In that group, he stood out as one of the most vocal critics of the constitutional status quo—and, perhaps, the most articulate.

Mario Dumont took a hand in the drafting of a strongly autonomist position paper authored by a Liberal Party commission headed by jurist Jean Allaire. The report called for the devolution from the federal government to the provinces of twenty-two powers that were either currently shared with or under the sole control of Ottawa.

The federal government of the future—as drawn up in the Allaire Report—would have exclusive control over only five policy areas: defence, customs, currency, equalization and the management of the federal debt.

At a party convention in March 1991, the Allaire Report became Quebec Liberal policy. The same month a Quebec commission headed by Jean Campeau and Michel Bélanger— two co-chairs with strong business credentials but opposite leanings when it came to Quebec sovereignty—handed in the conclusions of province-wide consultations on the constitutional way forward. Every party that held seats in Quebec both at the federal and provincial levels was represented on the commission. The report prescribed that, failing an acceptable constitutional offer to Quebec from the rest of Canada, Premier Bourassa was to hold a referendum to put the option of sovereignty to Quebecers not later than fall of 1992.

Legislation to reflect that recommendation was drafted and passed by the National Assembly in June 1991. But fourteen months later, in late summer 1992, with the deadline to put the question of their political future to Quebecers almost upon him, Bourassa jettisoned the Allaire Report's prescription for a massive devolution of federal government powers to Quebec as well as the plan for a vote on sovereignty. Instead, he decided to submit a new constitutional proposal to the province's voters.

The federal minister of intergovernmental affairs, Joe Clark, and the other nine premiers had spent the better part of a year and a half trying to hammer out a substitute accord to replace the dead Meech initiative. The Quebec premier joined those negotiations at the thirteenth hour—when the others had already arrived at an agreement in principle.

Robert Bourassa signed off on a deal in Charlottetown in late summer 1992.

That was the text he took to Quebecers for approval in a referendum scheduled for October 26 of the same year. That vote was to be held concurrently in Quebec and in the rest of Canada. Dumont and Allaire campaigned as Liberal dissenters against the Charlottetown Accord. They believed it came nowhere near Quebec's bottom line. After it was rejected they left the Quebec Liberal Party and set to out to create the ADQ. Allaire was initially chosen to be the new party's first leader, only to quit a month later for health reasons.

It was this unlikely chain of circumstances that led Dumont to fight a general election in 1994 as party leader before he'd reached the age of twenty-five, and to wake up a short year after that in his hometown of Rivière-du-Loup to the likelihood that, later that day, Quebec might take a first step on the way out of Canada.

As Dumont flipped between American news shows on the morning of the referendum, the importance of the day hit home. Quebec was at the centre of the international media radar and he had been instrumental in placing it there.

"I was only twenty-five years old. While I was not unaware of the importance of the episode or the stakes involved, watching the Quebec referendum being cast as the biggest international news across the world drove it home to me. My legs were shaking when I headed for the shower that morning."

The destination of his five-year voyage across Quebec's fundamental political divide seemed to be in sight but

Dumont was not certain how he felt about it. On that morning he was more preoccupied with not burning the bridges between Quebec and Canada than eager to venture forth into the *terra incognita* of an independent Quebec. And he found comfort in the notion that he was not the only pro-Yes leader who was so inclined.

As of the moment that he decided the ADQ would share the referendum tent of the Parti Québécois and the Bloc Québécois, Dumont took his cues from Lucien Bouchard. At times he shadowed the moves of his elder. At other times, he used the Bloc leader as a sounding board, to validate his own instincts.

In all instances, Dumont made sure that they were essentially on the same page. "If I had done something really stupid, I would have been stigmatized for it for a long time. But as long as Lucien was behind me, I told myself that I would be okay. If I aligned myself with his position, I would not come across as an extraterrestrial who was totally out of his depth."

On referendum day, the two might as well have been joined at the hip. On the morning of the vote, Bouchard flew from Montreal to his Lac-Saint-Jean riding to cast his ballot and then had his plane collect Dumont in the Lower St. Lawrence riding of Rivière-du-Loup.

They travelled back to Montreal together, only going their separate ways to prepare for that night's rally with their advisers. The two met up again at the Palais des congrès as the final results were coming in.

Despite being apart from Bouchard for much of the day, Dumont was uncomfortably aware that communications were difficult between the Bloc leader and Jacques Parizeau. At the best of times during the campaign, he himself had had little direct contact with the premier. Bouchard acted as the go-between. "All day I would call Lucien to find out what the plan for the evening was, and all I would hear at the other end of the line was a string of swear words as he vented his frustration over his inability to reach the premier."

In hindsight, Dumont describes the referendum day breakdown in communications between the leaders of the Yes camp in the hours before an expected victory as "the mystery of my life."

Mystery it might have been but surprise certainly not. With the polls showing the tide turning in favour of sovereignty, Bouchard and Dumont had anticipated the possibility that Parizeau would waste little time in shutting them out of the decision-making loop. They were resolved to be just as quick in keeping their foot in the premier's door—even if that might require threatening to kick it down.

Dumont says he and Bouchard spent the last week of the referendum campaign discussing what they might have to do to stop a victorious Parizeau from rushing Quebec headlong into independence. "For the two of us, it was clear that a victory would give us a mandate to negotiate. But we had discussed the possibility that after the referendum we might have to make some muscular moves to slow

Parizeau and prevent him from getting carried away by his sovereignist zeal.

"We had had conversations about the fact that it could become necessary to stop Parizeau if he seized the excuse that the federal government would not come to the table to throw everything overboard, abandon all plans for a negotiation and an orderly transition and simply break up from Canada on the basis of a 50-percent-plus-1 mandate and a unilateral declaration of independence."

Asked what those moves might have involved, Dumont says he and Bouchard were ready to play hardball to keep Parizeau in check. Specifically, they pondered throwing a wrench in Parizeau's bid for the swift recognition of a sovereign Quebec by key members of the international community, such as France.

"Imagine that a week after the referendum, two of the three leaders who asked Quebecers for a mandate to negotiate sovereignty tell the world that the premier does not see the way forward as we had imagined it. I wonder what the international community would have made of the news that two of the three leaders of the Yes camp did not interpret the result in the same way as Parizeau."

Many in the sovereignist community would have surely construed such an act as a betrayal, but Dumont felt he was simply being true to his objectives. "After a Yes I saw my role as that of a guardrail, especially with Lucien Bouchard onside. It seems Mr. Parizeau believed that once he had a Yes vote, Lucien and I did not matter because he would have had the law on his side. But the law is only one part of politics.

"Long after the fact, Parizeau has claimed that he would have picked up the ball and run to sovereignty. My sense is that this is highly dubious. A people cannot become sovereign without taking notice of the fact that it is happening. There is no doubt that Parizeau would have been the boss of the operation on the morning after a victory but a boss does not always get what he wants. Even a boss has to put up with constraints."

Of the leaders of the Yes camp, Dumont is the only one who arrived at the campaign's evening rally with a speech prepared in case of a defeat. He says he was far less certain than his two partners that victory was in the bag. He thought that Quebecers' natural reflex for prudence might have kicked in over the last stretch of the campaign and that some voters, once appraised of the strong Yes lead, might have retreated to their initial and safer federalist choice. "On the morning of the referendum, I thought that the possibility of a Yes victory was very, very real but that the opposite was more probable."

Where Bouchard and Parizeau had each composed only one text—pertaining to an expected victory and its aftermath—and ended up addressing their supporters from notes drafted on the fly—in one case with disastrous consequences—their ADQ partner had in fact brought four versions to the Palais des congrès. They dealt with a high and a low winning score for each option. But they were all based on a single common thread, and it dominated the remarks Dumont delivered that night when he prescribed that, notwithstanding the defeat of the Yes option, "the foundations of Canada have cracked. It is time to rebuild on a new basis."

Win or lose, Dumont's endgame was strikingly different from Parizeau's. The ADQ leader felt a close Yes vote would have fallen well short of the minimum threshold required to successfully achieve independence. "In democracy there is no other rule than 50 percent plus 1, but the complexities of the political life of a people go beyond a basic democratic rule," he argues.

From his perspective, a narrow sovereignist victory would have marked the end of the road, not for Quebec's place in Canada but rather for Parizeau himself. "In my mind, a narrow Yes vote would have made Canada as we know it implode, but that would have been followed within months by a big summit to patch it back together and draft a new confederation pact. Quebecers would then have been asked to support that pact. Parizeau would no longer have been in the picture. There would have been early elections in Quebec. I would have won ten seats instead of just my own."

After a Yes victory Dumont would have been happy enough to have Lucien Bouchard—his referendum mentor—steer Quebec into a re-confederated Canada as its premier. Chances are he would have joined his government.

CHAPTER 3

MASTER OF THE GAME: JACQUES PARIZEAU

A mong the main protagonists of the 1995 referendum, Jacques Parizeau—the leader of the Quebec Yes camp—was by far the least curious about how Prime Minister Jean Chrétien would react to a sovereignist victory.

In the early afternoon of October 30, the Quebec premier taped his speech—in French and English—to be broadcast that evening by the main Canadian and Quebec television networks if, as he expected, the Yes had won the vote. "It was a solemn text to show we were in control; that we knew where we were going and to appeal for calm," recalls the former premier.

Parizeau was untroubled by the fact that his first victory address to the nation(s) did not take into account the federal reaction to the referendum result. In fact, that was something he spent little time trying to anticipate. "It was simply out of my control."

Jacques Parizeau was well aware that Jean Chrétien might refuse to enter in secession negotiations with the sovereignist leadership on the basis of a slim Yes vote. Parizeau could not bank on even a noncommittal reaction from the prime minister. However Chrétien handled a loss, Parizeau figured that the initial federal response would be negative. "Knowing Chrétien, I had no illusions on that score."

In fact, Premier Parizeau expected no less than strenuous federal resistance to his victory, in particular on the matter of the economic and political partnership between Quebec and Canada that was so close to the hearts of his coalition partners, Lucien Bouchard and Mario Dumont.

Not only did Parizeau think Jean Chrétien would not want a role in the partnership movie but he also knew, based on the private talks that his team had held with the Reform Party, that Preston Manning was willing enough to discuss terms of secession after a Yes vote but not inclined to talk association—beyond the essential minimum—with a sovereign Quebec.

That, as it happened, suited Premier Parizeau just fine. Only under duress had he considered the idea of association in the first place.

In the 1980 referendum, the Yes camp had asked Quebecers for a mandate to negotiate sovereignty-association. Its calculation was that voters would be more inclined to buy into a step-by-step approach than an abrupt rupture with Canada. Parizeau was now convinced that the strategy had backfired. "We sold the notion of a future association with Canada to Quebecers so well that when a few politicians from English Canada said it was a non-starter, a lot of voters decided that without it sovereignty was also a non-starter."

He was determined to avoid falling into the same trap:

"I wanted to make sure that we would not be dependent on a partnership, that the fate of the sovereignty bid would not in any way be linked to our capacity to strike a political partnership with Canada."

When Lucien Bouchard had forced Parizeau's hand on the issue during the previous spring, the premier had given some ground to avoid the implosion of the sovereignist camp. But it was only a strategic retreat. He did not believe that a successful negotiation of the comprehensive partnership sought by his Bloc Québécois and ADQ allies was truly in the cards, and had made sure that, in the end, he would not need a cooperation agreement with Canada's order to march Quebec to independence.

Throughout the summer of 1995, he had let others flesh out the so-called partnership, agreeing as he puts it to "just about anything," as long as the timeline for its negotiation was not open-ended.

The 1995 Bill 1 on Respecting the Future of Quebec spells out the steps that the National Assembly is to take following a Yes vote. It lays out the broad terms of the association that Quebec would seek to maintain with Canada after secession. But success in those negotiations is not a pre-condition to declaring Quebec's sovereignty. Article 26 states that the partnership negotiations could not extend beyond October 30, 1996, without the consent of the National Assembly and that sovereignty could be proclaimed earlier if those talks were going nowhere. That section was ultimately all that mattered to Parizeau.

"I don't want to be mean, but I frankly did not care much what they put in the partnership. One can always hope for all kinds of things. I was told to be open-minded, to accept a partnership project, an association and I would answer: you can have everything you want as long as I have article 26."

To reassure his allies Parizeau had agreed to let an independent committee of wise men and women monitor the progress of any partnership negotiations. "The committee would have been there to ensure that everyone was negotiating in good faith. On that score I was probably the most suspect of all possible negotiators as I did not believe in the process."

But it was a double-edged sword for the proponents of a partnership, for in the not-unlikely event that Canada refused to negotiate on its basis or dragged its feet to the table, Parizeau counted on the committee to validate his decision to walk away from the process and go forward with a unilateral declaration of independence.

From the premier's perspective, the faster it became obvious to the rest of his coalition that the partnership talks were doomed, the better. "I knew where I wanted to go and at what pace I would get there depending on how much opposition I had to deal with in Ottawa and in the provinces."

Parizeau's best-case scenario was really that of a quick divorce like that undergone by Czechoslovakia in 1992. "The Slovaks said that they wanted to leave and the Czechs said good riddance. Within a year they had agreed to a sharing of assets and had gone their separate ways."

On October 30, 1995, no one was more prepared for a Yes vote than Jacques Parizeau. If there had been a sovereignist victory, Jean Chrétien, Paul Martin, Roy Romanow, Mike Harris, and even Lucien Bouchard and Mario Dumont would have had to improvise their way out of its immediate aftermath. But Parizeau had devoted the bulk of his adult life to preparing for this night. He had a three-metre-long shelf replete with studies on every possible issue involved in achieving secession from the federation. He could not imagine going on in politics if he lost. In fact, he knew that a defeat would terminate his career. He had made sure of it.

Earlier in the day, in addition to taping his victory address, Parizeau had given TVA journalist Stéphan Bureau an embargoed interview in which the premier had volunteered that if he lost the referendum he would leave politics. "After all those efforts, all those years, I was not going to stay on and start again. I had had more than my share of the pleasures of running a province. I was done with that."

Parizeau has always maintained that referendum day hubris did not lead him to trap himself into having to resign on the heels of a defeat; it had been his intention to quit all along, he says, and there is no reason not to take his word for it. Both his wife, Lisette Lapointe, and his veteran chief of staff, Jean Royer, concur. But it is also true that when he gave Bureau his interview, Parizeau—much like his advisers—was reasonably confident of victory. He expected many pieces of his sovereignty puzzle to have already fallen into place by the time their conversation was broadcast.

Within hours of the result, officials from the Quebec ministry of finance would have fanned out to the financial capitals of the world in an all-out effort to reassure the markets that the province was fiscally sound. "They already had their plane tickets," recalls Parizeau. A reserve of seventeen billion dollars had also been set aside to ensure Quebec could intervene in the markets to blunt the initial aftershock of the Yes vote on the province's bonds.

The premier was determined to avoid a repeat of the scenario that had unfolded after the election of the first PQ government in 1976. The province had initially been shut out of the North American financial markets, and as minister of finance he had had to find alternative lenders to finance the sovereignist government. He wanted to be sure that would not happen again on the day after the referendum. "It was essential to keep the markets open, to avoid a financial panic for that would have hurt us enormously with the public."

He had assembled a list of federalist establishment figures who had agreed to publicly lend credence to a Yes mandate and join the premier's call for a summit on Quebec's new challenges. A list of their names would be published in the province's newspapers the morning after the vote. The mayor of Montreal, Pierre Bourque, was also slated to make a statement along supportive lines.

The National Assembly would have been recalled within forty-eight hours to adopt a motion that would formally announce Quebec's determination to act on the referendum result. Parizeau headed a majority government. Even without the support of the Liberal opposition, the motion would pass. Further, the premier had been told he could expect some Liberal MNAs to break ranks with their party and support the government—as of course would the ADQ's Mario Dumont.

Parizeau expected, too, that in the House of Commons, Reform Party leader Preston Manning would simultaneously call for the resignation of the Chrétien government and for an election to give the next federal government a mandate to negotiate Quebec's separation. In France, the PQ's allies in President Jacques Chirac's government and in the French National Assembly were on standby, waiting for the Quebec National Assembly's declaratory motion so they could make their own gestures of support.

When it came to securing alliances within France's political circles, Premier Parizeau was convinced that he had done a complete end run on the Canadian government. If he won, he was certain the French would not let down the Quebec sovereignist movement.

France had a crucial role in Parizeau's post-Yes strategy. "Right from the beginning I thought negotiations with Canada would almost certainly fail. That is why I expended so much energy in courting the international community. For us, France was a major priority."

Indeed, if Parizeau, as he expected, was to move unilaterally to declare Quebec independent and do so sooner rather than later, his move would have to be followed up quickly by the recognition of some members of the international community, and he needed Paris—the seat of a first-world power—to take the lead.

And what of Lucien Bouchard—Parizeau's so-called chief negotiator—in all this? Well, as the former premier tells it today, staffing the negotiating team that the Bloc Québécois leader would head would have been one of the first items on his cabinet's post-Yes agenda, if only to make sure that he had his own people keeping an eye on his federal ally.

If he had been waiting by the phone to be consulted about who would make up the team, Bouchard would have (again) wasted his time. Premier Parizeau had his own ideas as to the group's makeup. "It would have essentially been people whom I trusted completely, drawn from the ranks of senior officials and from my own immediate entourage. I knew exactly which of them would be a good fit for the job."

Unlike Lucien Bouchard or Mario Dumont, Jacques Parizeau did not worry about a narrow mandate. He certainly did not think it could be used to deny his victory. "The simple majority rule was not a matter that was much debated back in 1995. That came later. In 1980 we had operated on a 50-percent-plus-1 basis and we took it for granted that it would be the same in 1995."

Parizeau's concerns about the Canadian reaction were of a different order. He worried about "irrational" moves such as sending the army into Quebec to affirm the authority of Canada over the province. "You would have the army marching down Sainte-Catherine Street in Montreal chanting: your vote does not count; your vote does not count. And then what happens? It would have been a ridiculous situation."

He also thought the opposition of some First Nations to Quebec's sovereignty bid could become problematic. Hydro-rich northern Quebec struck him as safe from the threat of partition. The Cree and the Inuit had signed off on the James Bay and Northern Quebec Agreement in 1975. He believed they would have a hard time making a case that they still held the territorial rights that would allow them to insist on remaining with the Canadian federation. But he knew they were going to make that case as forcefully as they could. And the story would have been different in the sections of southern Quebec where the Innu and the Mohawks who had signed no such treaties lived. "Sometimes I had the rather awful idea that I should just let the Canadian government continue to oversee those territories," he recalls.

But mostly Jacques Parizeau feared having his goal of sovereignty watered down at the Canada/Quebec negotiation table. "To get bogged down in the swamp of partnership negotiations, to have committees and subcommittees and proposals and counter-proposals spring out of the woodwork, and over that time to have people start questioning themselves about the process, for me that would have been a nightmare."

When all is said and done, Premier Parizeau's worst-case scenario, his "nightmare," as he calls it today, looked a lot like Lucien Bouchard and Mario Dumont's dream scenario.

It is useless to speculate how the simmering power struggle in the Yes camp would have played out in the aftermath of a victory. Two decades later, the debate over whose way forward after the referendum would have prevailed and with what consequences for Quebec and Canada is academic.

The fact that the meaning of a Yes vote was open to such divergent interpretations within the very group that championed sovereignty is both more troubling and more significant. Presumably, those differences would have faded in the face of a resounding Yes victory. But none of the three leaders expected better than a narrow win. Parizeau and Bouchard's best-case scenario was a 52 percent score, and Dumont thought that if the Yes did win it would likely be by an even smaller fraction.

As difficult as it might have been for the three to reconcile their differences in the heat of the campaign, that difficulty pales against how much harder it would have been to do so in the turmoil that would have attended a sovereignist referendum victory.

To put it mildly, the climate of suspicion that prevailed between the three leaders of the Yes camp was not promising. Indeed, had Quebecers been aware of the widening cracks in the sovereignist coalition as they headed to the polling stations that day, one can only wonder what voters would have made of it.

Dumont and Bouchard were convinced that Parizeau

was out to marginalize them, and with good reason. Parizeau had planned to oversee the sovereignty talks himself, with the assistance of a hand-picked team of bureaucrats and advisers. "The last person he wanted at the table was a politician, because he felt that if he sent a politician to the table, the federal government would be obliged to do the same," says Jean Royer, Parizeau's closest aide.

What Parizeau had in mind was a businesslike negotiation led by government technocrats who were used to working in an environment devoid of political passion. The talks would deal strictly with essential items such as the division of the debt, the disposal of the federal assets in Quebec, the means to ensure the free circulation of goods and people between Atlantic Canada and Ontario and the West. The two teams of officials would eventually hand their political masters a bloodless document on which to sign off.

Parizeau did not underestimate the strong negative emotions in the rest of Canada that stood to attend a Quebec Yes vote. On the contrary, his goal of a minimal Quebec/Canada association was partly based on his expectation that it would be difficult to accomplish anything more in the charged climate of the immediate post-referendum period.

"Bouchard wanted to reassure Canada by offering it the maximum in terms of association with a sovereign Quebec. Mr. Parizeau believed that Canadians would initially be in no mood to accept more than the minimum. He felt that if the two came around to the need for further association at some later date, they could deal with it at a time when emotions no longer ran so high," says Royer.

The premier had not sought Bouchard's input in his referendum strategy as much as had it imposed upon him. Lucien Bouchard had initially called for a post-sovereignty partnership with Canada in a speech to a Bloc Québécois convention. The premier, who was sitting in the first row of the audience, had been unaware that the proposition was coming until it hit him in the face. At the time Parizeau had had no other choice but to cave in or risk a civil war within his own camp, which would have dashed his plan to hold a referendum the following year, let alone win it.

But after a Yes victory he was set to surround Bouchard with his own people, and he counted on the independent committee that was to oversee the negotiation process to bolster his case that the partnership path was a dead-end street. Clearly, Premier Parizeau was willing to devote little energy to the Bloc leader's partnership bid.

Both as a former federal cabinet minister and as a Parliament Hill insider, Bouchard was more familiar with Canada's political networks than any of his partners in the National Assembly—including Parizeau himself. Before founding the Bloc, he had worked with some of the country's top public servants. And by the time of the referendum, the fifty-four Bloc Québécois MPs had been involved in parliamentary committees that dealt with every aspect of federal life—including international and fiscal policies—for two years.

Yet those who had been mandated by Parizeau to lay the groundwork for a future secession negotiation did not seek their expertise or Bouchard's advice. The Canada/Quebec association might have taken up more than half of the words of the convoluted referendum question, but translating the promised offer of partnership into a reality after the vote was simply not a priority for Parizeau.

The studies he had commissioned on the transition from Canadian province to full statehood suggested that the negotiation path to a partnership would have led to a high degree of integration between Canada and Quebec, so the premier dismissed his officials' analysis and sent them back to the drawing board.

When he spoke with us, Parizeau seemed unaware of the increasingly estranged referendum-day mindset of his coalition partners. But he made it clear that he would not have given up his control of the post-referendum agenda without a fight. "It was my prerogative to decide who would sit on Bouchard's negotiating committee and I had no intention of sharing it."

On the day after a Yes vote, he would not have lacked support within his government to stand up to Bouchard. The expectation within the upper ranks of the cabinet was essentially that the Bloc Québécois leader would have to march to the sound of Parizeau's drum.

Bernard Landry was deputy premier to Jacques Parizeau. They had both been part of René Lévesque's PQ government in the mid-seventies and they had each fought on the front lines of the first Quebec referendum in 1980. Landry had also had dealings with Bouchard before and after the creation of the Bloc Québécois. He had sided with the BQ leader in the debate over the introduction of a Quebec/

Canada partnership in the sovereignist referendum question the previous spring.

Landry readily acknowledges that there was little love lost between the PQ leader and his Bloc partner. "The least one can say about their relationship is that they did not connect easily. Bouchard was a little too enamoured of a post-referendum association with Canada for Parizeau's taste," Landry notes.

But there were also human factors at play: "A leader is by nature suspicious of anyone who might overshadow him," says Landry. The former premier himself admits that having to agree to Bouchard stepping up to the plate in his place at mid-campaign was "hard for the ego."

Landry points out that Parizeau had cause to see Bouchard as a potential threat to his authority and not just because the latter had prevailed in the partnership debate. "At the time Lucien had a lot of credibility even within the Parti Québécois; he was Saint Lucien. That is how he came to lead the PQ soon after the referendum."

For all that, Landry dismisses the tensions between the two and the referendum-day breakdown in communications between them as a mere case of campaign jitters. "If we had won, the joy of the moment would have taken care of such tensions. In the midst of jubilation there is no longer time for petty quarrels and recriminations."

In Landry's mind, there is no doubt that as of the moment that a Yes vote was in hand, Parizeau owned the driver's seat. He describes Bouchard's post-referendum role as that of "a very important accessory."

"Parizeau would have been triumphant. Achieving sovereignty was the fight of his life. It was even more the fight of his life than it was Lucien's, who had done a lot of other things before politics. He was the leader of the government of Quebec. He was the one who could negotiate in the name of the Quebec nation. Lucien is a democrat. He would have accepted that. He was not aggressive about it, just a little prickly."

From Landry's perspective, the mandate resulting from a Yes vote—even if won by a whisker—was not open to interpretation. "Quebec would have had a popular mandate to seek independence. We would have accepted nothing less and certainly nothing that would not have seen us have a seat at the United Nations. Given the magnitude of the change at hand, the internal tensions would not have had the chance to become a problem."

Landry believes one should not read much into the fact that Bouchard had so little inside knowledge of the moves undertaken by Parizeau in preparation for victory—including the premier's decision to set aside the prep work that would have paved the way to keeping intact a lot of what Canada and Quebec already had in common. According to the former deputy premier, until the vote was in, the premier and the BQ leader simply had more immediate and more pressing matters on their respective plates.

As for Dumont, he was the least of Landry's worries. "At the time, Mario did not have the stature of a statesman. He had founded a party that was marginal. He was not and still is not an intellectual. He has never had deep thoughts about these issues. Given all that, he would not have been much of a problem."

Landry's optimism that the Yes camp could maintain a united front in the days and weeks after a victory and his take on the *rapport de forces* between the three leaders stand in stark contrast with the narrative put forward by Dumont and Bouchard.

Dumont's testimony leaves little doubt that Bouchard was a willing participant in the discussion of moves liable—if it had come to that—to have created chaos within his own camp in the aftermath of a Yes vote. It is equally clear that Dumont would not have contemplated taking on Parizeau alone.

It is plausible that the years that have elapsed since the 1995 referendum have exacerbated the differences between Dumont, Bouchard and Parizeau. After the defeat they all went their separate ways. Parizeau resigned as premier on the day after the vote. Had he not quit, his referendum-night speech would have haunted him for the rest of his tenure. But the existence of the pre-taped TVA interview makes it clear that the referendum defeat rather than the controversial spin that the premier put on it on the night of the vote drove his decision.

As he had planned all along and confirmed with his wife on referendum night, Bouchard did not linger on Parliament Hill and very soon took the helm of the PQ and the Quebec government. In the years that followed, his relationship with Parizeau continued to sour as it became obvious that the new premier was failing to come up with the so-called winning conditions for a victorious referendum. Bouchard focused the energies of his government on eliminating the deficit, at the expense—in the perception of many péquistes—of pursuing sovereignty.

Shortly after the 1995 vote, Dumont called for a ten-year moratorium on the sovereignty debate. Bouchard, Landry and Parizeau all scoffed at the suggestion and Dumont took his distance from his former partners. He and Bouchard campaigned against each other in the 1998 Quebec election.

Neither Dumont nor Bouchard believe that sovereignty will be achieved in the foreseeable future. That clearly does not break the heart of the former ADQ leader.

In 2007, Dumont led his party to a forty-one-seat second-place score and the title of official opposition. But in an election held eighteen months later, the ADQ was pushed back to third place and he resigned. Today he is a television host.

In 2012, the ADQ merged with the Coalition Avenir Québec. François Legault, a former PQ minister, was the driving force behind the creation of the CAQ; yet for all his past sovereignist credentials, it is almost certain that his party would not join the Yes camp in the event of another referendum.

As for Bouchard, since retiring as premier a decade ago he has regularly suggested that Quebec had more pressing matters to deal with than that of its constitutional future.

Parizeau, for his part, has stuck to his staunch sovereignist convictions, growing estranged from the Parti Québécois in the process. None of his successors—including Bernard

Landry who held the post for two years between 2001 and 2003—has approached the quest for sovereignty with Parizeau's single-mindedness. But then none of them was handed a Quebec/Canada crisis that raised nationalist passions to a fever pitch in Quebec in the way of the constitutional wars of the late eighties and early nineties.

PART 2

THE QUEBEC NO CAMP

CHAPTER 4

THE SCULLERY MOUSE: LUCIENNE ROBILLARD

Lucien Bouchard, Mario Dumont and Jacques Parizeau were not the only Quebec politicians who were in something less than a party mood once the referendum results were in. Over at the Métropolis the No camp welcomed its razor-thin victory in a less than orderly fashion, and in the curious absence of Lucienne Robillard, the Liberal MP tasked as the intermediary between the Quebec No forces and their federal allies. The uneasy alliances that had been struck between federalist partners in the face of the sovereignist threat were fraying as quickly as those that had tenuously held the Yes camp together. It did not help that the result was so close that the victory carried with it the sour smell of defeat.

The teams that made up the Yes triumvirate had spent the evening in the same venue as each other and yet their leaders had barely spoken. A few blocks away at the Métropolis, difficulties in communicating were compounded by the 200 kilometres between the prime minister and key protagonists of the No camp waiting in Montreal to speak to the outcome.

Jean Chrétien had watched the results from his official residence at 24 Sussex Drive. Win or lose, he was scheduled to go live on television that night from an Ottawa studio. But the exact timing of Chrétien's appearance left the Tories crying foul. Jean Charest had barely started his speech to the federalist supporters gathered at the Métropolis when the networks cut him off to go to Chrétien's address.

To this day Charest loyalists believe that it was a deliberate slight, engineered by Chrétien's inner circle to deprive their Tory rival of the opportunity to remind the country—in prime time—of the major role he had played in Canada's hour of need. They remain convinced that Liberal strategists worried that Charest would cash in on the positive reviews he'd garnered over the course of the referendum campaign and use them to contrast his inspired performance with Chrétien's near defeat.

For their part, former members of the prime minister's palace guard maintain that the incident was merely the result of an accident in timing. They say that it was a pure coincidence that Chrétien took to the air before Charest had time to deliver his remarks. That may be true, but if so the prime minister's advisers were on a lucky streak. Cutting into Charest's speech was only one of two somewhat happy political coincidences for the Liberal prime minister and his team that night.

In the confusion that attended the federalist victory rally at the Métropolis, few noticed that Lucienne Robillard was missing in action. The prime minister's televised address covered up her absence in the Montreal speaking roster.

The missing Robillard was Chrétien's lead minister on the referendum. But she had another distinction. Among those in the 1995 federalist camp, she was considered the most likely to accept a Yes vote at face value and, further, the most inclined to interpret the close federalist result as a call for a radical change in the Canada/Quebec relationship.

On her way out of a cabinet meeting a few weeks before the vote, Robillard had been asked by the media how her government would react to a close Yes vote. She recalls, "I said that, regardless of the result, we would respect the will of Quebecers."

In the event of a Yes victory, that made Robillard a potential time bomb for her own government. On referendum night, it was in the power of the Quebec federalists who had fought for Canada in the campaign trenches to turn a slight pro-sovereignty mandate into a more definitive one. Should they signal that they were willing to rally behind a narrow Yes verdict, it would be that much harder for the federal government to deny or even to appeal it. And if Chrétien's own referendum emissary took the lead and legitimized the sovereignist victory, the prime minister would be left with precious little elbow room to fight his way out of a Yes vote. As it turned out, events conspired to moot the issue of Robillard's reaction to the referendum outcome. She never made it to the Métropolis.

Tory leader Jean Charest and Quebec Liberal leader Daniel Johnson were on site to watch the results come in. But Robillard spent the evening closeted with her staff and her security detail in a suite of the downtown Montreal

Sheraton hotel. "It was only after the fact that I discovered that Charest and Johnson had both gone straight to the Métropolis," she says.

Twenty years ago, federal ministers were not systematically handed speaking notes and ordered to recite them as if by rote. The regimen under which today's ministers are expected to parrot the government line had yet to be implemented in a comprehensive way. Robillard was slated to speak on behalf of the federal government later that night at the Métropolis, but she was not handed a text by Chrétien's spin doctors. Given the uncertainty of the outcome, they would have had to provide her with two versions of a speech, one for a victory and another for a defeat. It is highly unlikely that Chrétien would have wanted to share with Robillard his intentions in the event of a federalist defeat. Their political relationship had never been based on full disclosure—as the minister found out when federal decisions about referendum strategy were taken without her knowledge during the campaign.

Weeks earlier, her stance on respecting the referendum outcome had drawn an agitated reaction from PMO officials. Robillard had quickly inferred that her position must have been at odds with that of the prime minister. "After I said that, I was hauled into Chrétien's office. He only asked me what I had said and what words I had used. But from the reaction, I deduced that if the Yes won with 52 percent or 53 percent, we would not accept it. But the prime minister and I never specifically discussed it."

On referendum night, the instructions issued to Chrétien's lead referendum minister boiled down to waiting for the green light before heading out to the Métropolis. "No matter what the result is, you are not to say anything in public until Chrétien has spoken. The boss will speak and then you will." Robillard says she was told this over a series of phone calls with Ottawa that evening.

The minister did not have her usual bodyguard with her that night. During the referendum campaign the RCMP had taken over the task of ensuring her safety, and by the time she was finally cleared to leave for the Métropolis, the agent in charge of Robillard's detail told her that havoc had broken out in the streets of Montreal. If she insisted on going to the rally, he said he could not guarantee her safety. "I sat and watched the speeches on television. That is when I realized that both Charest and Johnson were on hand while I was not. I was very angry."

Robillard might have been even angrier had she been aware that Radio-Canada was reporting that downtown Montreal was relatively calm in the hours after the referendum result and certainly a lot more calm than in the aftermath of a hockey series. When asked if she felt that she had been (gently) sequestered that night, Robillard answered that it had not crossed her mind at the time. Nevertheless, her narrative, as she presents it two decades later, seems designed to foster that conclusion.

If Lucienne Robillard had found her way to the Métropolis and spoken from the heart on the night of October 30, 1995, chances are her speech would have echoed the address Mario Dumont had given earlier in the evening at the Yes rally and not the careful address to the nation of her prime minister.

Dumont had joined the Yes camp because he believed it was the only possible route to a Quebec-friendly overhaul of the Constitution. Robillard had gone the other way and joined Jean Chrétien's government with a similar objective.

In his first public comments that night, Dumont had called for profound changes to the workings of the federation. Robillard's read of the result was not substantially different. "I was very naive when I first came to Ottawa. I had arrived on Parliament Hill with the illusion that the federal government had the power and the will to change the relationship between Quebec and Canada for the better. It was only after the referendum that I realized that change was not in the offing.

"I was part of a majority federal government but to effect the kind of changes I imagined for Canada, you needed more than that. In any event, Mr. Chrétien had no appetite for those changes. And to achieve them, the provinces would have had to be ready to come on board."

On the night of the referendum, Robillard had not had much time to take stock of the country's political dynamics. The winner of a by-election in February of the same year, she was a Parliament Hill rookie who had yet to celebrate her first anniversary as a federal politician.

Robillard had earned her political stripes in the provincial arena. She had served as a senior minister in Quebec's Liberal government—holding major portfolios such as health and education—until she lost her seat in the 1994 election that had brought the Parti Québécois back to power.

Some politicians have politics in their blood. Their passion for the game borders on addiction and it becomes a lifelong calling. Robillard was not predisposed to become a political lifer. By her own admission, she was not an eloquent public speaker or at least not one who would ever be in the league of Lucien Bouchard or Jean Charest. Her capacity to command an audience was limited.

"When I lost my provincial seat in 1994, it was not a personal disaster. I had been in politics for five years and throughout my career I had always operated on a five-year cycle. I figured I would branch out into something else. I decided to give myself six months before accepting one of the offers that were coming my way. Until I received a call from Ottawa, I had never considered federal politics as an option. If I said yes, it was because a referendum was coming. For me, it was a fundamental issue. The invitation was one I could not refuse."

The provincial law under which referendums are conducted in Quebec stipulates that the leader of the opposition in the National Assembly is the leader of the No camp. The prime minister has no formal role in the Quebec process. So Chrétien had recruited Robillard at Quebec Liberal leader Daniel Johnson's suggestion, because he needed a minister who was familiar with the ways of the provincial Liberals and could close the gap between him and Daniel Johnson. None of his Quebec MPs really fit the bill. The one who came the closest was André Ouellet, a veteran minister who had served as a political fixer in Quebec under Pierre Trudeau. But Ouellet was foreign affairs minister. He was abroad much of the time, which made him a poor fit for a domestic mission like the Quebec referendum campaign.

Marcel Massé, Chrétien's minister of intergovernmental affairs, was a career bureaucrat who had served as Clerk of the Privy Council under the previous Progressive Conservative government. His forte was policy, not raw politics. He wouldn't suit the job either. As for Paul Martin—the other senior Quebec minister—he was immersed in the war on the federal deficit. Moreover, he and Chrétien had had serious constitutional differences in the past, most notably on the Meech Lake Accord. Chrétien opposed it on the grounds that it would seed more disunity in the federation while Martin believed that it would restore harmony between Quebec and the rest of the country. Neither man trusted the other's approach to Quebec.

Overall, the federal Liberal caucus was weak on representation from the heavily francophone ridings that make up the province outside Montreal and where the sovereignist camp expected to fill up on referendum votes. Together the Bloc and the PQ totally dominated those regions.

To make matters worse, the relationship between the Quebec federal and provincial Liberal clans—which was not cozy at the best of times—was close to an all-time low.

The provincial and federal Liberals, or at least the Chrétien side of the federal family, had fought on opposite sides of the Meech Lake debate. There was little personal rapport between Chrétien and Daniel Johnson.

The hope was that Robillard's presence would help smooth the Ottawa-Quebec federalist waters and inject some much-needed cordiality into the relationship between the two leaders. In hindsight, the latter at least was an impossible mission. Robillard famously remembers a Chrétien/ Johnson dinner that she had pushed for in the hope of getting the prime minister and premier closer on referendum strategy. It achieved little except to exhaust her. "When I left I was as tired as if I had spent the evening washing floors."

Overall, Lucienne Robillard remembers her referendum experience as a lonely trek on a very rocky path. With her roots firmly planted in provincial soil, her transplant into federal politics did not take. "For a Quebec Liberal, the federal Liberals are not family. And when one finds oneself in Parliament there is a big culture shock. When I first heard Preston Manning speak, when I heard the speeches of the Reform Party, I wondered if I was still in Canada. My Liberal colleagues were not overly friendly. I had been parachuted into a safe seat (Westmount–Ville-Marie) by the prime minister. Many of my caucus colleagues were wondering what I had that was so special that it warranted that Mr. Chrétien go out of his way to get me elected.

"On top of that, I was unfamiliar with the body language of the federal government and with its implicit protocols. I did not know how the federal apparatus operated. I had no real personal links with any of those around me, in the cabinet or the caucus. I did not really know André Ouellet or Marcel Massé except by reputation and they did not know me. If I had known then what I know today about the federal machine, about the way it works and the people who run it, I would not have accepted Chrétien's invitation."

By referendum night, Robillard had fallen out of the circles that she was supposed to connect. Johnson's people had become convinced that she was a conduit to nowhere and preferred to deal with Chrétien's advisers directly. Her own government seemed to have just as little use for her. Some of Chrétien's strategists felt that she was spending more time making Johnson's case to them than pushing the Quebec Liberal leader down the preferred federal path. "It was the most difficult part of my political life. I felt I was sandwiched between Quebec and Ottawa. A lot of things were put in play without me being aware of them. I was on the road at least half the time. A lot was decided in Ottawa while I was on the road. I was crisscrossing Quebec and making speeches and I did not have ears and eyes in high places."

With polls showing that the Yes had built a substantial lead in the last week of the campaign, she—like Daniel Johnson—had pushed for a strong signal of change to come from Chrétien. But she had no direct input in the make-or-break speech the prime minister finally gave at the Verdun arena in the dying days of the campaign, and she came away from it unimpressed by his deathbed overtures to the recognition of Quebec's "distinct" character. Overall, Robillard felt Chrétien's promises fell short of the mark.

Just before the speech, one of the prime minister's top aides had taken her aside and told her that the speech would make her happy. "He said: We are promising distinct society. I answered: Is that all?"

She was away when some of her cabinet colleagues from outside Quebec set out to organize what became known as the federalist love-in at the end of the campaign. Held on the Friday before the vote, the massive rally brought thousands of Canadians from every region to downtown Montreal, many on the dime of the federal government or of corporate Canada and in violation of Quebec's referendum spending law. "I did not give my blessing to the love-in. Nor did other Quebec ministers. It was very risky and we had undertaken to respect the Quebec law. I still think it hurt us more than it helped."

On the morning of October 30, Robillard was bracing for a sovereignist victory. But those who feared that she would repeat her earlier statement that the federal government would respect the will of Quebecers—as weakly as they might end up expressing that will—need not have worried.

Again like Dumont, Robillard did not believe that a bare majority was sufficient to set Quebec's secession in motion. "I have always thought that intelligent sovereignists such as Lucien Bouchard would never set out to achieve sovereignty on the basis of a bare majority mandate. Anyone with a head on his shoulders would know that it was a recipe for a crisis. I believe that sovereignists like Mr. Bouchard have always thought that it might be doable at 52 percent, 53 percent, 54 percent, but not at barely 50 percent."

Nor did she plan to resign in the face of a close Yes vote. "Many key federal posts were in the hands of Quebecers, but I for one did not ever think that we would not be the team to face the music. But I did not know what we would have done. Back then I was never apprised of any post-Yes game plan. I was in regular contact with the Privy Council. I was part of the strategy committee of the No camp along with the Quebec Liberals. I never heard the issue of what we would collectively have done or said in the event of a federalist defeat discussed in any way."

Very much like their rivals in the other camp, the tenors of the No side in Ottawa and in Montreal had done nothing to ensure that they would sing from the same songbook if the Yes prevailed that night. And when their side beat the odds and secured the narrowest of victories, they were equally unable to agree on what meaning they would give to the result.

CHAPTER 5

THE KID IN THE CANDY STORE: JEAN CHAREST

When he woke up in North Hatley in Quebec's Eastern Townships on the morning of the 1995 referendum, Tory leader Jean Charest feared that Canada was about to go into free fall. If the Yes prevailed, he and his aides had determined that he would try to hit the pause button in an attempt to prevent Jacques Parizeau from fast-forwarding Quebec to independence. But he knew that it was impossible to rewind a broken tape, at least not without mending it. And his role, if it came to such a delicate operation, stood to be severely limited.

That morning Charest could easily imagine that the referendum vote would mark the beginning of the end of his federal career. And in fact it would do just that, but not for any of the reasons the Tory leader could guess on that day. In all the speculative scenarios involving a Yes victory that he had in mind, none offered much hope of a brilliant future for a federal MP who held a seat in a province whose voters had decided that they no longer wanted to be represented in Parliament.

Even in Sherbrooke—a riding that had sent him to the House of Commons through the best and the worst of Tory times—Charest had found his pleas for Quebec to continue as a province of Canada to be a hard sell. "I felt the country was in the balance. I feared that going back on a Yes vote would be like putting toothpaste back in a tube. A sovereignist victory would set all kinds of events in motion over which we would have no control. I did not think a Yes vote would be just a passing phase. I felt it was a real step down the road to a break-up."

Of the four federalist leaders in the House of Commons, only Charest had been on the ground in Quebec non-stop throughout the referendum campaign, pleading the case for federalism in parish halls, seniors' homes and at chamber of commerce lunches.

Reform leader Preston Manning did not speak French and some of the policies of his party—starting with their commitments to phase out official bilingualism and severely restrict access to abortions—were not helpful to the federalist forces in progressive Quebec. He stayed well out of the fray.

The referendum campaign coincided with the final stretch of the NDP's leadership campaign. Alexa McDonough replaced Audrey McLaughlin at the head of the federal New Democrats only two weeks before the Quebec vote. In 1995, few federal New Democrats boasted a profile in Quebec, where neither the former nor the new NDP leader was a household name. When first elected in the Yukon to the House of Commons, outgoing leader Audrey McLaughlin had obtained a dispensation from the party line and was allowed to vote against the Meech Lake Accord. She had felt that the accord would hurt the interests of women and Northern aboriginal voters, but her position would have been seen as hostile in Quebec, if noticed at all.

The NDP caucus did boast two Quebec-friendly faces in Saskatchewan's Lorne Nystrom and British Columbia's Svend Robinson. Both were fluent in French and well versed in the province's politics. But they had thrown their hats in the NDP ring against McDonough and had spent most of the referendum campaign occupied by their own bids for party leadership.

As for Jean Chrétien, it had been decided early on that he would limit his participation in the referendum to a few select appearances.

Charest had mixed feelings about coming to the end of the campaign road and not only because he was uncertain of its outcome. With the tide turning against the No side in the second half of the campaign, he had emerged as the star of a federalist camp desperate to offset the eloquence of Lucien Bouchard with some passion of its own. His plea to Quebecers not to give up on their passport was one of the rare acts of the No camp that got the normally subdued federalist audiences onto their feet.

The 1995 federalist lineup did not lack for competent performers but it was desperately short of inspirational public speakers. No one in the No camp came close to Charest in terms of sheer campaigning skills. In time he would come to be recognized as the best Canadian campaigner of his political generation.

By the morning of October 30, it would be fair to say that among the leading figures of the federalist team, Jean Charest was one of the very few who had found the experience exhilarating. "From 1993 to 1995 I was nowhere; I was on no one's radar. When the referendum campaign got under-way in '95 I was like a kid in the candy store. I was getting a lot of coverage. But as soon as it was over, it was curtain time for me."

In a federal election held two years before the referen-dum, Charest's Progressive Conservative Party had been decimated. As one of only two Tory survivors and with former prime minister Kim Campbell defeated in her own riding, Charest was left to pick up the pieces of his shattered party. The defeat left the Tories ten members short of the minimum required for a party to be officially recognized in the House of Commons. Charest, who had been deputy prime minister to former leadership rival Kim Campbell at the time of the 1993 federal election, found himself fighting for even crumbs of speaking time in the House.

As a consequence of the Tory fall from grace, Charest—even as he became a marquee performer for his side—was essentially relegated to the strategy sidelines. Over the first half of the campaign, when the going was good for the fed-eralist side, Prime Minister Chrétien and his brain trust had seen no need to bring the Progressive Conservative leader to the decision-making table. And when the things soured for the No camp and Charest's stump skills became essential, his authority within the campaign did not rise in concert with his celebrity.

Over the final week before the vote, Charest watched Chrétien scramble to regain the initiative for his side. With the clock ticking on the federalists, the Tory leader sat in Verdun's arena and watched the prime minister reverse himself on the need for constitutional accommodation for Quebec and advocate its recognition as a distinct society. It was a move for which the prime minister—in his days as a Liberal leadership candidate and as leader of the official opposition in the House of Commons—had never had any appetite.

Chrétien had supported the Charlottetown Accord negotiated by Brian Mulroney and the premiers in 1992 that included a section dealing with Quebec's distinct status. But he participated in the referendum campaign that followed its negotiation as quietly as possible. The federal Liberals remained deeply divided over the issue and former prime minister Pierre Trudeau never reconciled himself with the distinct society concept. He had made a fiery speech against the Charlottetown Accord during the federal referendum campaign to decide whether that agreement would alter the Constitution, and at the time his words, not Chrétien's, were still considered marching orders by many a federal Liberal.

Until his speech in Verdun a few days before the 1995 vote, Chrétien had always been careful to keep his distance from the distinct society idea. When the prime minister changed course, Charest, much like Lucienne Robillard, was not impressed. "I was not consulted. I saw it as an admission of failure. Everyone knew that it did not come from the heart, that it was a move dictated by the difficult circumstances of the campaign. I could not see how, over the long term, that approach could yield results. I had defended distinct society at the time of the Meech Lake debate but that was in a context where it would have been seen as a major step forward."

In the desperate heat of the last stretch of a losing campaign, Chrétien was promising Quebecers constitutional change; but Charest expected, with good reason, that even if the prime minister meant to be true to his word, he would not be able to deliver.

Left to his own devices in the lead-up to the referendum, the Tory leader had consulted widely as he tried to stake out a position for his party in the upcoming Quebec battle. Charest knew that he could not just cheerlead. The Progressive Conservative Party—if it was ever to rise out of the ashes— had to offer Quebecers something different from the Liberal agenda. But that something also had to be doable.

He asked a dozen experts from different academic and political venues for their suggestions. The group included former federal mandarins such as Gordon Robertson and Roger Tassé. Ron Watts—the Queen's University scholar who had been drafted into service by Brian Mulroney for the Charlottetown constitutional round—was asked for input as was political columnist Gordon Gibson—a former Liberal leader in British Columbia. Stéphane Dion—who would be asked to join Chrétien's government as his unity point man after the referendum—was one of a handful of Quebec academics who also provided Charest with advice.

The result was a predictably mixed bag of suggestions, but a briefing note prepared for Charest shows that the group agreed on at least one fundamental point: "constitutional reform was extremely unlikely in Canada in the near future."

According to the same précis, there was consensus on the notion that the Yes could not win a majority if Quebecers believed that there was an alternative to separation that was not the status quo. But Gordon Gibson qualified this postulate: "The first characteristic of any credible third option is that it must be defined in the interest of the rest of Canada [ROC] and *not* to please Quebec. While the result must be acceptable to everyone, Quebec included, the political mood in ROC is such that anything designed for Quebec will be suspect, and not saleable." As the previous installments of the constitutional saga had demonstrated, there could be no reform of federalism without substantial provincial and popular support. If Gibson was right—and there was plenty of evidence to support his thesis—a distinct society proposal along the lines of Chrétien's referendum promise belonged squarely in the category of constitutional non-starters.

As leader of the smallest caucus in the House of Commons, Charest was in no position to make substantive promises on the referendum campaign trail. In fact, he could not promise much of anything. That was the prerogative of the prime minister. But some ideas put forward by his group of experts stuck in his mind and he eventually followed up on them.

Among the highlights of the experts' proposals were variations on the theme of a new intergovernmental forum designed to bring the federal and provincial governments together around a more cooperative concept of federalism. Almost a decade later, Charest's first national initiative as Quebec premier was to persuade the other provinces to create a Council of the Federation. The hope was that such a forum would incite the country's first ministers to act less like so many solitudes and more like the co-participants in a federation. In spite of the council, interprovincial cooperation remains a work in progress.

By the evening of October 30, there was no longer time for constitutional considerations. A looming Yes victory was the uninvited elephant in the federalist backrooms of the Métropolis. Everyone was trying hard to pretend to ignore it, in the fervent hope that it would vanish.

Unlike Preston Manning and Jean Chrétien, who both waited for the results in Ottawa, Charest was in Montreal— in close contact with Daniel Johnson and his team of advisers. Like the Quebec leader of the No camp, Charest was not privy to Jean Chrétien's plans in the event of a Yes vote. He says there had been no approaches, covert or otherwise, on behalf of the federal government to broach the issue of the Tory response to a federalist defeat or to seek input on an appropriate federal reaction, and no attempt to ensure that there be a common federalist response to a Yes vote. Charest recalls discussing the issue with no one outside his party. "I would remember if someone had come to me and said: Jean, if there is a Yes vote tonight, it would be important to not concede anything."

Over the years, Charest has come up with a theory to account for the radio silence maintained by Chrétien and his advisers. "It may be that they decided it would be more effective to wait for me to be under the immediate pressure of a Yes vote before suggesting a course of action than to give me three days to hash out with my advisers whether I should play ball with a defeated Chrétien. We were in full improvisation mode. I presumed that some people in the Privy Council had worked out some tentative scenarios and that we would be apprised of them if need be in the wake of the vote."

As far as Charest was concerned, he was on his own that night. Until advised otherwise, he had to assume that if things went south for the federalists, it would be every man and woman, or in this instance every leader, for himself.

Thinking ahead to a possible close Yes vote, he did know that he would not call for Chrétien's immediate resignation. (As a federal leader from Quebec himself, he could hardly have asked the prime minister to quit without putting himself in an awkward position.) "Chrétien's immediate resignation would only have added to the turmoil. It would not have been in the interest of either Quebec or Canada to have the prime minister quit on the night of the referendum. It would have been better to have him stay long enough to have the question of who would speak for Canada resolved."

But Charest was convinced that he—like Chrétien—would have been vulnerable. And he was convinced that the Liberal government as it was, top-heavy with Quebecers, would not endure for long. "In the event of a Yes vote, the legitimacy of the government of Canada would have been in question. And if one was an MP from Quebec as I was, could one continue to speak for Canada? There is little doubt that one would have had to reconfigure the federal government."

A majority of voters in both Chrétien's and Charest's ridings voted yes in 1995. That fact would have made their respective positions as federal leaders even more untenable if their side had lost.

Even if an uncontrollable chain of events stood to be unleashed in the wake of a Yes vote, Charest was not going to rush to conclusions about the meaning of the result: "My instinct would have been to buy time, not to say that it was over on that night. Faced with the unknown, I would not have thrown in the towel. I would not have challenged the result, but I would have wanted to step back and take the time to see how things were playing out."

Like Lucien Bouchard in the opposing camp, Charest focused on only one speech in preparation for his side's evening rally and it dealt with a narrow Yes win. Drafted on his instructions by political consultant Bruce Anderson, the text reflected Charest's determination to wait to see how the post-Yes dust would settle.

That draft speech conceded nothing. Two decades after the fact it reads more like a declaration of war than the remarks of a leader whose side has just lost a decisive battle. "If I truly believed that the majority of Quebecers had opted to separate from Canada, I might be tempted to concede that the dream [of a united Canada] is over. But what many of those Quebecers who voted yes have said tonight is not that they want to leave Canada but that they, like millions of other Canadians, want to change Canada. They want to be able to reclaim it as their own," Charest's draft states.

About Bouchard and Parizeau, the winners of the night, the text notes: "I do not doubt their commitment to the cause of separation. But even they cannot interpret this result as a mandate to take Quebec out of Canada. For my part, I will pause briefly, listen to what the people of Quebec and Canada are saying as they reflect on this outcome . . . My love for Canada, my love for Quebec, and my belief that our greater destiny lies in staying together have not been diminished by this evening's results any more than it was by the failures of the past . . . We cannot and will not choose to do otherwise than continue to fight to keep Quebec within Canada."

If he'd had to deliver that speech, Charest might have opted to soften some of its more combative language. After all, his own constituents in Sherbrooke had voted against his cause.

In spite of the fighting words that Anderson had prepared for him, Charest says he was not confident that a referendum verdict in favour of sovereignty, even if it resulted from a deeply split jury, could be easily overturned. He expected

Jacques Parizeau to waste no time in seizing the initiative so as to take advantage of a routed federalist camp. He feared the Quebec premier would make moves that would quickly harden minds in the rest of Canada.

"I thought Parizeau would go ahead with a UDI rapidly. That France would be willing to support Quebec in short order. There were political actors in Quebec and outside Quebec who would have seen those moves as a licence to make some hardline gestures of their own. Parizeau would have set events in motion over which he would have had no control."

Charest was never among those who believe that Jean Chrétien could just have shrugged off the result—even one achieved by the narrowest of margins. "A Yes vote is a defeat. Someone has won and someone has lost and the loser cannot just act as if he had won and go back to business as usual. Chrétien could well have said that there was nothing to negotiate, that the question was not clear. But we had spent the campaign arguing the opposite and hammering that a vote for the Yes was a vote for breaking up with Canada. We had run our entire campaign on the premise that a vote for the Yes was a decisive vote. It would have been difficult to go back on that."

As federal leader, Charest had his ear to the ground in the rest of Canada. He doubted that Canadians had the stomach or the inclination for a long trench war to keep Quebec in the fold. "The attitude in the rest of Canada would have been to bring things to a conclusion. People did not like the idea that it would be a drawn-out episode, that it would just go on indefinitely. The political class would have felt pressure to get on with it. That's the sense I got when I travelled to other parts of Canada. It is the kind of feeling that no law can define or circumscribe."

When Charest finally left the Métropolis that night, much like the majority of his fellow politicians, and most pundits, he thought that Quebec and Canada would soon face another hour of reckoning. He feared that if Lucien Bouchard were in complete command of the Yes side for that rematch, it would be the sovereignists' to lose.

Charest was sure of something else that night, that Bouchard would want to leave the House of Commons sooner rather than later. He had never made a secret of the fact that he was not going to stick around after a referendum defeat. If someone had suggested that the Bloc Québécois leader would be replacing Jacques Parizeau in very short order, Charest would not have been surprised.

But never in his wildest calculations did Jean Charest figure—as he pondered the very mixed, very sobering results of the Quebec vote—that the referendum campaign had sowed the seed of his own transplant to the provincial arena. Those seeds would germinate so rapidly that Charest—as Daniel Johnson's successor as Quebec Liberal leader—would be facing Bouchard three years down the road—not in another referendum or on the federal campaign trail, but in a provincial election.

After the referendum, Charest never again found himself on the winning side of a vote against Lucien Bouchard. In his first provincial duel in 1998, Charest lost the election to his former Tory cabinet seatmate but his Liberals won the popular vote. That was the first of a post-referendum string of federalist moral victories that included a similar federal Liberal victory in the Quebec popular vote, this time by Jean Chrétien over the Bloc Québécois in the federal election of 2000. Two decades later, it is those subsequent victories rather than their unimpressive referendum finish that allow the pro-Canada leaders to claim that they had truly won the night on October 30, 1995.

CHAPTER 6

DOCTOR NO: DANIEL JOHNSON

I t is usually easier to be gracious in victory than in defeat. But that is not true in the case of Daniel Johnson—the Quebec Liberal leader who led the No forces in the 1995 referendum. Of all the interviews we conducted for this book, the one we did with Johnson was by far the most adversarial. Although he agreed readily enough to talk, he then spent the bulk of the discussion telling us what he was determined not to discuss. Toward the end of the interview, he wondered whether it had even been worth our while to meet him. We, in turn, wondered why he had agreed to go through the motions of having a conversation that took ninety minutes out of his presumably busy schedule. Rehashing the memories of the referendum episode seemed to fuel a simmering anger that time has apparently not abated. His side in the referendum ultimately came out on top on October 30, 1995, but Johnson obviously draws little satisfaction from the experience. He makes it sound like a spectacular waste of his and everyone else's time.

On referendum night, Jacques Parizeau's lifelong dream suffered what could yet prove to be a fatal hit; and Lucien Bouchard brought the sovereignty movement tantalizingly close to its goal only to see the tide recede under his feet. Yet it is Johnson—leader of the winning camp—who oozes bitterness when he reminisces about the campaign.

To this day he seethes about the fact that the Parti Québécois put the question of Quebec's political future to its citizens for a second time, calling repeat referendums "a debilitating tragedy." He adds: "One goes into politics to help a society move forward, not to bring it to the edge of a cliff to then ask it to jump."

From his perspective, the PQ might as well be bent on sabotaging Quebec just to satisfy its ideological whims. Theirs, he says, is "an imposed agenda that people will eventually always reject and that can only weaken Quebec's negotiating position versus Canada."

What he leaves unsaid is that it was the Liberal government of Robert Bourassa that first held a match close to the secession fire by putting another sovereignty referendum on the Quebec agenda after the Meech Lake Accord failed in 1990. In the year after the accord died, Bourassa introduced a bill in the National Assembly prescribing a sovereignty referendum in the fall of 1992 should no acceptable constitutional offer emanate from the rest of Canada before that deadline.

Bill 150 was passed into law on June 20, 1991, with the support of Johnson, who was then a minister in Bourassa's Quebec government.

———————

Since the 1995 referendum, Paul Martin has lived through the heartbreak of losing the job of prime minister after serving only half the four-year span of a regular mandate and after having hankered for the post for over a decade. When we interviewed him, Jean Charest had just lost power after a decade as premier in Quebec. Over the previous year he had struggled with a major social crisis that had seen thousands of Quebecers take to the streets in protest against his government for weeks on end. Raymond Chrétien, a long-time diplomat and Canada's ambassador to Washington during the period of the 1995 referendum, had to deal with wars, famines and—in the case of Rwanda—a genocide. All of these men described the 1995 referendum as the most intense experience of their diverse careers. Not so Daniel Johnson.

When Johnson talks about leading the 1995 No camp he sounds more annoyed than anything else. It is a task he looks back on as an imposition. "I did not seek to be the leader of the No camp. I am not sure one is necessarily more proud of what one achieved in imposed circumstances rather than what one accomplished of his own volition. To ask the question is to answer it."

Despite the ups and downs of the No campaign, Johnson says he never doubted that he would win. "I was always confident we would win. I did not think Quebecers wanted to vote yes to a question that would have spelled the end of the Canadian experiment." He admits that Lucien Bouchard's ascendance in the middle of the sovereignist campaign changed the dynamics of the No camp for the worse. "It was as if the sun had stopped rising in the east," he says. He describes casting aside Jacques Parizeau in mid-campaign as a "crass" strategy. For the leader of the No camp, the Quebec/Canada partnership put forward by the Yes camp did nothing to enhance the sovereignty project: "All that association stuff, the currency discussion, the integration scenario, no one had ever shown me the beginning of an interest in the rest of Canada for such a project or for accommodating a separate country within its institutions. The chances of success of such a bid are between zero and nil and therefore of no interest for Quebec."

But as confident of victory as he claims to have been, Johnson still prepared a speech to deal with the contingency of a referendum defeat. He will not say whether it was a concession speech or one along the lines of Jean Charest's combative remarks. In contrast with Charest, who worked on a draft speech with a team of advisers, Johnson's former aides insist that he did not brief or consult them on his intentions. Speaking on background, none believes that the Liberal leader was going to accept a Yes vote at face value. His own words suggest as much.

For instance, about Jean Chrétien's probable reaction to a federalist defeat, Johnson says: "In hindsight, I think he would have said the question was not clear enough. I would not have been against that. It would have been a good response. I had long believed one does not break a country up over a recount. It is not acceptable to change the life of a people, its place in the world, on such a basis."

One party insider suggests that Johnson would rather have resigned as Liberal leader than participate in the PQ's bid to lead Quebec to sovereignty. Another says he is "100 percent" certain that his boss would not have conceded the victory to sovereignists, that his instinct would have been to say that the mandate was not strong enough and that Quebecers should reconsider. But that former aide also believes that Johnson would have urged Canada to hold out its hand to Quebecers and offer to renegotiate the workings of the federation— particularly, but not exclusively, the sharing of powers between the federal and provincial governments.

What is more certain is that Johnson's role after a Yes vote would have mattered most in the hours immediately following the result. As the defeated leader of a destabilized federalist camp, he would have seen his audience in and outside Quebec quickly shrink. On the morning after a Yes vote, Daniel Johnson would have woken up in a federalist minefield. It was highly unlikely that he would walk out of it with his party or his leadership in one piece.

Thinking ahead to a referendum victory, Parti Québécois strategists knew that few developments would enhance the credibility of their mandate to negotiate secession, in Canada and abroad, more than the sight of the defeated federalist champions supporting the winning side. If the result turned out to be as close as the polls predicted, Premier Parizeau would need some degree of bipartisan support to solidify his victory and heal the deep division that had split Quebec into two camps.

He did not expect ready support to come from the Quebecer who served as Canada's prime minister or from federal Tory leader Jean Charest or even from Jean Chrétien's half-dozen Quebec ministers. Jacques Parizeau counted on forces from the rest of Canada—within the Liberal government and outside it—to neutralize the federalist Quebecers toiling in Ottawa and replace them quickly with their own people.

But ideally the premier wanted the Liberal opposition in the National Assembly to sign off on the verdict within a week of the vote. If Parizeau was going to succeed in bringing Quebec to independence within a year, Daniel Johnson and his party had to fall in line behind his government, or at least be rendered impotent. To help make that happen, the premier was set to hold a political knife to the throat of his Liberal opponent. If Johnson would not lead his forces over to the sovereignist camp, other federalists would do it for him.

John Parisella was one of Johnson's top advisers. More importantly from the perspective of Jean Royer—Parizeau's tireless chief of staff—Parisella was the Liberal strategist with whom Royer enjoyed the most cordial relationship. On the day before the vote, he got in touch with Parisella to serve notice of the government's post-referendum intentions. With polls showing that the Yes camp's lead was holding and with only twenty-four hours to go, Royer wanted to sound out what role the Liberals saw for themselves in the aftermath of a sovereignist victory.

If the Yes won, the PQ government planned to introduce

a motion in the National Assembly that would validate the result at the first opportunity. Royer was fishing for any assurance that the opposition would support that motion, as well as guidance on what terms would make the motion palatable to the greatest number of Liberal MNAs. "We did not expect the Liberals to applaud the result but we did want them to acknowledge it. I wanted Parisella to give me his assessment as to whether his party would agree to such a motion. I did not expect unanimous Liberal support but I wanted to know if we could hope for a majority [of them]."

The exchange between the two started off with the tone of a goodwill mission. But soon the gloves came off. Parisella still had cause for hope. The fluid polling numbers suggested that a voting-day reversal of the pro-sovereignty trend was still in the cards, and it was premature, or at least counter-intuitive, for either side to lay down its weapons. Further, Parisella had no mandate from Daniel Johnson to engage in what could only have been construed as concession negoti-ations. If word leaked out that he had, it would damage federalist morale just when the No camp needed all hands eagerly on deck to get the vote out. So Parisella was not inclined to venture onto the slippery ground of discussing post-referendum scenarios.

Royer says he could sense that he was getting nowhere but he knew that would change quickly if, as he expected, the results went his way the next day. At that point Johnson's inner circle would need to have a serious discussion about their party's options, so Royer gave Parisella some arguments that could force the Liberals to come onside, elaborating in particular on a card that Parizeau had told us he was ready to play on the morning after. "We had assurances from a number of leading federalist figures in Quebec's civil society that if we [the Yes camp] reached 52 percent the next day, they would come out, not to say it was a great result, but to accept that it was the verdict of the Quebec people."

Royer did not share his entire list of prospective morning-after converts with Parisella, but he did give him a taste of the calibre of people he was talking about. Gérald Tremblay, one of Johnson's former provincial cabinet seatmates (and a future mayor of Montreal) was on the list, as was Liberal MNA Yvon Picotte. Cardinal Jean-Claude Turcotte, Montreal's highest-ranking Roman Catholic cleric, and Pietro Rizzuto, a Liberal senator with strong links to the Chrétien clan in Quebec, were also in the mix. In total two hundred opinion makers from all quarters of Quebec's civil society had agreed to have their names published by the PQ in every major newspaper on the day after a Yes victory. The ad—which Parizeau and Royer described as ready to run—did not mention secession or separation. But the signatories did recognize the sovereignist referendum victory and called for a summit on the challenges that faced Quebec in its aftermath.

It was not a threat that Johnson, as leader of Quebec's federalist forces, was prepared to take kindly, but it did illustrate how tenuous his place as official opposition leader would become if his side lost the vote. The subtext of the conversation between Royer and Parisella was straightforward enough: if Johnson did not willingly support the victors' post-referendum plans, enough Liberals would vote with their feet that he would be left with a mere shell of a party.

That was the part of the Liberals' post-referendum picture that suited Royer's interests best and he naturally brought it to Parisella's attention. But there was a flip side. Again speaking on background, former members of Johnson's inner circle readily acknowledge that, yes, the Quebec Liberal caucus might have imploded under the pressure of a sovereignist victory. But they also suggest that party unity would have been harder to maintain had Johnson agreed to go along with the PQ script. From their inside perspective, a narrow Yes vote was a lose-lose proposal, regardless of what tack Johnson chose to take. If he opted to cooperate with Parizeau and the PQ, the ultra-federalist wing of his caucus would not follow. On Montreal's West Island, referendum-day support for the federalist option turned out to be so massive as to border on monolithic. Many of Johnson's MNAs hailed from such staunchly federalist ridings. They and their constituents would have balked at the notion that their party could associate itself with an operation designed to sever Quebec's provincial ties with Canada—especially on the basis of a narrow result. But if Johnson refused to play ball with Parizeau, he stood to lose the nationalist section of his caucus. With some high-profile federalists—including some caucus colleagues—ready to lead by example and move behind Parizeau, the mat stood to be pulled from under the Liberal leader's feet within days if not hours of a sovereignist referendum victory.

The post-Meech Liberal Party that Johnson led was not the same one that Robert Bourassa had brought back to power in the mid-eighties. Since then the party had lost part of its nationalist wing to the constitutional wars. A significant part of it had fled the party with Mario Dumont and Jean Allaire at the time of the 1992 Charlottetown referendum. As a result, on balance Johnson's former aides still believe that validating a Yes vote would have been the greater risk for both his leadership and the future of the party. One Liberal strategist who was close to the scene over those years estimates that if Johnson had declined to sign off on a Yes victory, no more than ten Liberal MNAs would have crossed the floor to the Parti Québécois. That, however, may be an optimistic estimate.

Johnson himself will not say what he would have done if he had found himself between the rock of his federalist creed and the hard place of a Yes vote on the night of October 30. The quasi-ultimatum that the other side tried to put to him in the dying hours of the campaign is just one of many referendum developments that he scoffs at when he is asked to reflect on his experience as leader of the federalist forces in 1995. But he is equally scathing about some of the campaign developments on the federalist side of the ledger.

Johnson's relationship with Chrétien was as strained as that of Lucien Bouchard's with Jacques Parizeau. The former Quebec Liberal leader does not have a specific recollection of the dinner that so exhausted the conversation skills of Lucienne Robillard, but he does depict some of his campaign-related exchanges with the prime minister as comparable to "eating in the same restaurant at the same time and ordering the same thing but doing it at different tables." Johnson makes no secret of the fact that he and his federal allies came at the referendum exercise from perspectives that were not always easy to reconcile. "For Chrétien, it was in or out of Canada. Fair enough for a Canadian prime minister. But how do you integrate that in a campaign that pits Quebec nationalists against other Quebec nationalists?"

Since Quebec's referendum law placed the provincial opposition leader in charge of the No camp, in theory Jean Chrétien had to at least run his plans by Daniel Johnson. The latter is well aware that expecting a prime minister to defer to a provincial opposition leader on an issue that involves the future of the country fails the test of political reality. It is at a minimum a recipe for serious turf wars: "In a coalition the government of Canada is going to act like the government of Canada, not like a partner. Chrétien and his team might have liked to take over the No camp but I would have liked to see them try!"

One of the worst days of the No campaign featured a public disagreement between Chrétien and Johnson. On the campaign trail, the Quebec Liberal leader spoke of his wish that the prime minister would promote the constitutional recognition of Quebec as a distinct society before the referendum vote (which Chrétien had not yet done). From New York, where he was celebrating the fiftieth anniversary of the United Nations, the prime minister shot back that he was interested in talking about separation, not the Constitution.

There could not have been a worse time in the campaign for the two main figures of the federalist camp to squabble in the media over constitutional change. The federalist forces were struggling and the episode almost sent the entire federalist narrative into a tailspin. A few days later Chrétien relented, changed his strategy and promised that a No vote on October 30 would be followed by action toward recognition of Quebec's distinctive character.

It was not the last time the two allies found themselves at odds over strategy. Johnson still fumes about the pro-Canada rally that brought thousands of Canadians to Montreal to mark the culmination of the No campaign. He thought it was a harmful distraction. In its lead-up, Johnson had his people call as many Canadian corporate offices as possible, urging them to desist from offering free transportation or other services to people who wanted to come to Montreal and participate in the massive show of support for federalism.

He felt he wasted precious time shaking hands with some of the groups who travelled to Montreal. "I should have ignored them," he says nearly two decades later. Of the many politicians who attended the rally, Mike Harris seems to be among the few who made a lasting impression. Johnson says he remembers that the Ontario premier sported a white-and-blue cap!

On a more serious note, Johnson expresses no regret about the outcome of the last referendum—even if it was never followed by the constitutional change that he and his party hoped for at the time. "I consider that I stopped

Quebec from going down a path that was not in its interest. It is simply not in our interest to separate. Knowing the toll a Yes vote would have taken on our economy, our society, we are better off today than we would have been if the Yes side had prevailed."

But his tone suggests that two decades later he still pines for the decisive federalist victory that he initially had cause to expect, a victory so resounding as to put an end to Quebec's existential debate. In his political photo album there is an empty space for the trophy fish that got away.

After the referendum, Daniel Johnson never again led his Liberal troops to victory. By the time the next Quebec election came around, three years later, he had resigned to make way for Jean Charest. The federalist elites in and outside Quebec had come to see the Tory leader as the most likely to hold Bouchard and the threat of another referendum at bay. They pushed hard on both Charest and Johnson to make the jump happen. As it went for Claude Ryan, who led the No camp in 1980, the 1995 referendum was the only campaign that Johnson would ever win as leader and it was a bittersweet victory at best.

PART 3

THE FEDS

CHAPTER 7

THE CANADIAN COUSIN: SHEILA COPPS

The second-in-command in Jean Chrétien's Liberal cabinet spent the make-or-break evening of October 30 alone in her Ottawa living room. As then–deputy prime minister Sheila Copps remembers it, the only conversations she had as she sat glued to her television were with her brother. He was watching the same news special from his Quebec home and they would phone each other "every five minutes" to compare notes. No one else—from the senior levels of the government or from the prime minister's office—rang her phone, not even when the Yes built an early lead and it looked as if the night was lost for the federalists. If the tide had not turned, the country's deputy prime minister would have found out how Jean Chrétien had been planning to handle a Yes vote at the same time as the millions of other Canadians who, like her, were watching Quebec's political drama unfold from afar.

Looking at a chart of who was who in the federal cabinet, someone unfamiliar with the ways of the Canadian government might be taken aback to know the deputy prime minister would not be at the side of the prime minister on a night as crucial as this. But Ottawa watchers would not be in the least surprised. For the better part of four decades, control and influence have inexorably seeped away from the elected MPs who sit in the cabinet and in the House of Commons and toward the unelected inner circle of the prime minister.

On the watch of every prime minister from Pierre Trudeau in the seventies onward, knowledge and the power that it yields have become more and more concentrated in the hands of the political advisers who staff the PMO. Under Jean Chrétien, the Quebec issue in particular was handled by an even more restricted circle within the PMO perimeter. As under Trudeau and Brian Mulroney, managing Quebec was largely the purview of a tight circle of advisers who for the most part hailed from the province, and strategic information about the task was often dispensed on a need-to-know basis.

Over his final months as a member of the federal government, despite his role as Quebec political minister, Lucien Bouchard was himself not always aware of Brian Mulroney's plans on the Meech Lake front. One night a Bouchard aide even called *Le Devoir* to ask if staff would share any inside constitutional information. Bouchard was trying to get a handle on any last-ditch federal-provincial manoeuvres with which the prime minister hoped to salvage the accord—and if the call to the newspaper was any indication, the Quebec minister was failing to pry satisfactory answers from his own government. (Until recently in Canada, no file was more insulated from the mainstream of the cabinet and the government than the so-called unity one.)

Sheila Copps notes that there has always been less to the title of deputy prime minister than meets the eye. It is more honorific than influential and is officially vested with little actual power. A deputy prime minister may stand in the place of a prime minister who is absent from question period. But no actual government department is attached to the role and the title earns those who hold it no special consideration from senior government officials. "The bureaucracy tends to hate the idea of a deputy prime minister because it is a role that does not exist in the parliamentary tradition," she says, speaking from first-hand experience.

Since 2006 Stephen Harper has done without a deputy prime minister. Few Canadians have noticed—and even they would be hard-pressed to argue that a government without a deputy prime minister is somehow missing an essential piece. As often as not the utility of naming a deputy prime minister has been political. The title can send a message to a given region of the country or to a specific constituency that it matters to the government of the day.

Copps's appointment came in the wake of the 1993 defeat of Kim Campbell, Canada's first female prime minister. Furthermore, the NDP under Audrey McLaughlin—that party's first female leader—failed to keep the twelve seats required to retain official party status in the House of Commons. That election had dealt a harsh blow to the hopes of those who thought women were about to finally take a more equal place in Canada's political major leagues.

Appointing Copps as deputy prime minister was a reward for her loyalty to Chrétien throughout his opposition years; it was also a signal that the new prime minister intended to bring more women to the corridors of federal power. Up to a point, Jean Chrétien did deliver. On his watch more women were appointed to the Senate, the Supreme Court bench, the upper levels of the diplomatic service and to the select ranks of the officers of Parliament than under any of his predecessors.

Still, the levers of political power remained in mostly male hands. In 1995, that failing hardly distinguished the federal government from its provincial counterparts, but today the political gender gap between Ottawa and the provincial capitals is more striking. In 2013, half of the provinces—including the four biggest—were being run by female premiers. But back in 1995, elected women were still very much confined to support roles within their parties and governments, regardless of lofty titles bestowed upon them.

There had been no woman at the federal-provincial table for the multiple constitutional rounds that preceded the 1995 referendum, and the strategy rooms of the Yes and No camps in Quebec were overwhelmingly filled by elected and non-elected men in suits. The lone woman in the thick of referendum decision-making hailed from the federal public service and not the elected ranks of the federal or Quebec governments. Jocelyne Bourgon was appointed to the top public service job of Clerk of the Privy Council shortly after Chrétien's arrival in power and her tenure covered the referendum period.

Lucienne Robillard—even as lead referendum minister for the federal government—spent more time out of the decision-making loop than in it. Over the campaign, she had her strings pulled in contrary directions more often than she cares to remember. The popular and bilingual Copps, doubly hobbled by her status as a non-Quebec politician, did not even have a specific referendum role.

She spent the campaign preaching to the converted. For the better part of a month, the deputy prime minister travelled Quebec—in places where encounters with voters not already sold on the merits of federalism were few and far between. On those rare occasions when she did meet undecided voters, it happened despite the best efforts of the No camp.

The mission of her Quebec handlers, as Copps came to understand it, was to put non-Quebec politicians on low impact make-work projects. "They were afraid of being attacked for having brought people from outside the province to win the referendum." Stuck on what she describes today as the "C-circuit" of the No campaign, she was sent to Quebec City—the overwhelmingly francophone home of the National Assembly—to address an English-speaking group. Another day, on a pit stop in Montreal's Rosemont neighbourhood, she found a grand total of two No camp volunteers waiting for her in a small committee room and, under such ignominious circumstances, too many media persons for comfort.

To save face, she pretended that the plan had always been for her to head out from there and go glad-hand subway riders. With the cameras in tow, she proceeded to the closest Metro station. "I looked like an idiot," she recalls.

It was not until the dying days of the campaign that she finally got a shot at speaking to a very large federalist gathering. On the Friday before the vote, she joined cabinet colleague Brian Tobin on a stage erected on Montreal's Place du Canada to greet and warm up the large crowd that had assembled for the big pro-Canada rally.

Thousands of people had travelled from every region of the country to voice their support for a united Canada. But the power was cut and the microphones went dead just as Copps was about to speak. "Someone in the sound crew had decided that since we were outsiders to Quebec we should not be speaking."

There was nothing personal in the relegation of Copps to the sidelines. She was relatively popular in the province, but as a rule the Quebec No camp strived to keep out-of-province politicians out of the hair of those that it deemed fit to win them votes. Very few non-Quebec politicians made the cut and Chrétien himself, although prime minister and a Quebec MP, was not on the A-list of his provincial partners.

His participation in the campaign was a matter of heated debate both in Ottawa and in Quebec. Chrétien's own cabinet didn't unanimously support his increased role during the last week of the campaign, nor were they all sold on his plan to promise in Verdun that the constitutional change many Quebecers craved would not be a casualty of a federalist win.

Copps had been a steadfast supporter of Quebec's recognition as a distinct society. She had taken Jean Chrétien to task over it and over the Meech Lake Accord when she had run against him for the leadership in 1990. She fully supported his change of position on the constitutional issue itself and the decision to play a more active role in the last week of the referendum campaign. "I told him that he should do it; that if he did nothing it would come back to haunt him if we lost. Even if it did not work, he would at least feel that he had tried to do something to turn the tide."

But on the issue of planning for a federalist defeat, the prime minister did not seek Copps's advice. And even as a Chrétien loyalist, she is far from certain that he could have survived a Yes result for very long. "He would still have been elected democratically, but would that have been enough to salvage enough moral authority to continue on as prime minister? Had he failed to convince Quebecers to choose to stay in the federation, his authority would have taken a hit. There would have been a lot of finger pointing. The biggest finger would point at the prime minister."

Copps is not certain that a Yes vote would have led to the demise of Confederation. But she is equally uncertain that it would not have. She does believe that a Yes would have necessitated some negotiated change to the relationship between Quebec and Canada. "The question was not as clear as it could have been. The result might have been challenged in a variety of venues but I assume that if Quebec had voted yes, we would have had to discuss a new Quebec/ Canada deal. The referendum question alluded to such a deal. There would have been a chance to negotiate something. I assume we would have tried to forge a different relationship."

When asked how the constituents that she knew best, the Hamiltonians who had elected her repeatedly since the early eighties, to Queen's Park and then to the House of Commons, would have reacted to a Yes vote, Copps feels that fatigue with Quebec would have set in sooner rather than later.

She does not think the voters of her riding would have had a lot of patience for a prolonged period of suspense and uncertainty. "There comes a time when people ask themselves: If Quebec really wants to separate, why would we stop them? If it is something they so take to heart, let's negotiate and become separate countries, because the whole process is becoming repetitive."

But then she qualifies that assessment, wondering if perhaps it is not too cool-headed. "It is easy to say twenty years after the fact that, yes, we would all have negotiated our own deal, but in the spirit of the time the craziness could have come out. There are those people who cannot rationalize their way through such a result.

"It is possible that on the night of or on the morning after a Yes vote, emotions would have dictated something else. Because when one feels rejected, it is like a divorce. It can become very ugly. Even if there are good grounds to divorce, the beginning of the process often feels like the rubbing of a raw wound."

Like many of the federalists who fought in the trenches of the Quebec referendum, Copps came away from the experience with frustrations that were not offset by the satisfaction of the razor-thin victory. "The thing that I found that was not resolved is that in the fight for a country, some of the partners in that country do not even have a right to be heard. I wanted to fight for my country and I was basically told to fuck off and go away. On the one hand we were told that it was a matter for Quebecers to resolve; on the other we were expected to know what to do if the Yes won."

For her remaining decade in federal politics, Copps was spared having to resolve her place, and those of other interested non-Quebecers, in another referendum. But she continued to play a role on the unity front—as it was then known in federal circles.

In the wake of the referendum, federal strategists—directed by Jean Chrétien—set out to launch a flag-waving campaign. Part of the rationale was to make Canada more visible in Quebec. But the government was also seeking to respond to the wave of patriotism that had swept over the rest of Canada in the lead-up to the Quebec vote. It needed to address the feeling of exclusion and powerlessness that many non-Quebecers had felt as they had watched their country on the brink of what could have instigated a total break-up.

These days many Liberals lament the rise of what they perceive as government-driven jingoism under the rule of

Stephen Harper. Some of them see the Conservative attempts to highlight the monarchy and the country's military history as an attempt to import American-style patriotism to Canada. There is some truth to this assessment. But if one had to trace back the steps that led to a federal government engaging in the business of reshaping the national psyche along its preferred lines, one would find that the post-referendum Chrétien Liberals—with their ambition of pasting the Maple Leaf flag all over Quebec—got there first.

Part of the federal Liberals' post-referendum objective was to address the near-fatal deficit of emotion in the No campaign by engaging their sovereignist foes on the field of symbols. In particular, Chrétien felt that the presence of the Canadian flag needed reinforcing across Quebec. He wanted the Maple Leaf to be celebrated by the federal civil service on Flag Day (February 15) and ordered the distribution on demand of thousands of flags. The days when the battle for Canada in Quebec took place behind a cloak of invisibility were presumably over

Most of Chrétien's Quebec ministers were wary of the approach concocted by their government. They had spent the referendum campaign arguing that there was no contradiction between being a proud Quebecer and a proud Canadian. They had insisted that the rest of Canada prized the Quebec difference. A sudden emphasis on waving the Maple Leaf struck them as counterintuitive.

As minister of heritage, Copps was put in charge of the flag initiative and she acquitted herself of the task with zeal. It missed the mark with all but staunch federalists. Most

Quebecers—especially among the soft nationalists the Chrétien government was trying to win over on a permanent basis—saw the program as part of a flag war. Many were suffering from referendum fatigue. The last thing they wanted was to again be pulled in opposite directions by their two governments and their politicians. The subliminal message that many decoded was that Ottawa wanted them to choose between Quebec and Canada.

The thinking behind the flag program was a variation on the theme that inspired the ill-fated sponsorship program. The misuse of that program's funds for personal and partisan purposes led to a crippling scandal for the ruling Liberals and contributed significantly to their exile from power in 2006.

Ironically Copps dodged the sponsorship bullet for the same reasons that she was marginalized over the course of the referendum. Like the 1995 campaign (and unlike the flag initiative), the day-to-day running of the post-referendum sponsorship program was largely contained within a Quebec group of for-hire political operators, civil servants and marketing agencies.

A decade after the referendum, a poll found that the majority of Quebecers would rather not wear either the federalist or the sovereignist label. If the federal flag program had succeeded in any way, it was in turning a number of Quebec voters off flags altogether.

As for Copps, her own standing in the province never totally recovered from her proactive role in the flag initiative—or at least not for as long as she was still in politics. It overshadowed her otherwise popular record as heritage minister. Talking up the flag in Quebec marked her as an outsider—a Canadian cousin from away whose overt patriotism was out of synch with the province. In 2003 her leadership run against Paul Martin would attract little more Quebec support than her previous try in 1990.

CHAPTER 8

FROM DOVE TO HAWK: BRIAN TOBIN

On a chessboard, the fate of the king determines the outcome of a game. Once that piece is taken out, the game is over, no matter how many other pawns are still standing. But in politics the rules are different. The king is a disposable figure; it is vulnerable to attack by pieces of the same colour.

At the time of the 1995 referendum, Quebecers surrounded Jean Chrétien. Ministers such as Paul Martin at finance, André Ouellet at foreign affairs and Marcel Massé, who acted as federal go-between with the provinces, all hailed from Quebec and they all occupied crucial squares at the centre of the Liberal chessboard.

The political infrastructure of the prime minister's office was essentially built out of the same material. In Jean Chrétien's Ottawa, a lot of power was concentrated in the hands of Quebecers—especially on the unity file.

For the morning after a Yes victory the knights, rooks and bishops from the rest of Canada who filled up the other Liberal squares had a radically different configuration in mind. After a Yes vote the prime minister would have had to come to terms with those ministers. If need be, they were ready to checkmate their own king to advance to more strategic positions.

Had the federalist camp lost the referendum, Brian Tobin—then the minister of fisheries and oceans but also a long-time Chrétien loyalist—would have been one of those ready to lead the charge. "My good friend Jean Chrétien would probably not be happy with me but the reality is that under the British parliamentary system we don't elect prime ministers. Stephen Harper was not elected prime minister of Canada; neither was Jean Chrétien.

"They both were leaders of parties that won majority governments. Therefore as leaders of those parties, they get called up as leader of the party to form a government, but they have never been elected in the way of the president of the United States. You're only the boss if you can say to the governor general that I have at my back the majority of the House. But because it seldom happens people forget that a caucus in the British parliamentary system can remove a leader, including a prime minister.

"So the reality is that in a circumstance like that [a referendum defeat], the leader's traditional ability to dictate a course of action, even to dictate who shall comprise the cabinet and what role each will play, is limited by a need to listen and to comprehend reality. The normal discipline and the power of a leader to be unfettered vanish. They are not weakened. They are gone."

Tobin did not arrive at his take in isolation. In the days

before the referendum, a group of ministers had gathered in the private room of an Ottawa restaurant to discuss morning-after scenarios. It was an invitation-only informal event attended by more than half a dozen cabinet ministers. Most held front-line posts in the Liberal government. None of their Quebec colleagues made the guest list. The ROC ministers who were asked to come all showed up. The most glaring absence from the guest list was that of deputy prime minister Sheila Copps. Like Tobin, she was considered a leading Chrétien loyalist. But she figures she did not get invited because she was out of town when the meeting was hastily set up. No notes were taken. It was not the kind of conversation that would be put in writing on ministerial briefing paper.

"There were no decisions taken. It was just a decision on the part of a number of ministers to get together and at least acknowledge that the outcome was very uncertain. All of us were ministers from outside Quebec. At that time, the key folks who would have had responsibilities to negotiate were all Quebecers. But there is a simple reality that Quebecers would have to face in the event of a Yes vote and it is that the notion that there would be a bunch of Quebecers negotiating with a bunch of Quebecers is false. It would never happen.

"Constitutionally, Jean Chrétien was the prime minister. That is true. But if there began to be a negotiated settlement of the question, the negotiation would be done, the dialogue would be done, by folks who were looking in an unvarnished way at the interests of both sides."

Chrétien's ministers did not discuss his abdication that evening. But they did talk about negotiating possible terms of separation with Quebec on the basis of a Yes vote. "We had engaged in the referendum on the basis of 50 percent plus 1. You cannot change the rules afterwards. In my judgment if you actually got a clear win (52 to 53 percent), you entered in a negotiation about how we rearrange the country. My sense at that point was that we had played by those rules and we had to be ready."

The knives they sharpened in anticipation of a possible Yes vote were not meant to be pointed at the prime minister, or at least not directly. But the ministers present essentially agreed that with the government bleeding and opposition sharks circling a weakened post-Yes Liberal Party, their Quebec colleagues who held key portfolios would have to be redeployed to less strategic positions or, in some cases, simply made to walk the plank out of cabinet.

"You would clearly have had a reorganization of the federal government to reflect the reality of a decision, had it gone the wrong way. There would have been a realignment of people who had responsibility."

Tobin does not spell it out, but based on the picture that he paints, after a referendum defeat Chrétien would have been more like a hostage to his ministerial knights than a king protected by them. "I don't think he would have offered to quit or to leave and I don't think caucus would have asked him to, but I think the caucus and the cabinet would very much have wanted to be engaged in what the strategy was on a go-forward basis. I don't think simply saying we are going to keep everybody in his or her current spot and carry on would have been advisable or possible. I would just leave it at that."

Tobin assumes Chrétien would have acknowledged a defeat but left its interpretation for later—after the prime minister had had a chance to take stock of the new reality with his caucus and cabinet. "On referendum night I would have expected Jean Chrétien to say: There has been a vote for a new relationship between Quebec and Canada. But the question was not particularly clear and so the result is unclear. There will have to be a dialogue between the government of Canada and the government of Quebec to try to interpret what it was that the people of Quebec voted for. We know that they voted for change. We acknowledge that they voted for a new arrangement. That arrangement is yet to be determined."

Over the last week of the campaign, Tobin and some of his colleagues had turned their minds to where they would take the Quebec/Canada conversation. They knew they did not want leadership of that conversation to rest with the Quebecers in their government. "It was very clear that if we entered into that kind of a dialogue, post-referendum, that it could not be done by a group of Quebecers speaking for Canada because Canada would not accept it.

"I would not even assume that the prime minister in his role . . . would have been at risk, but I am saying that all the key slots were in the hands of Quebecers. That was good for a referendum campaign, but had the result gone the other way, there would have had to be some changes to reflect the reality that Canada would have to be at the table as part of this difficult negotiation as to how we move forward post-referendum.

"We could be of the view around the cabinet table and deep in our hearts that those Quebecers were the best people, but practically, in reality, it just could not happen. There would not have been on the part of the rest of Canada a position that we are negotiating from sentiment."

They also knew that they did not want to leave the terms of engagement up to the Quebec sovereignists who would sit across the table from them. "It would not be a one-step process where the government of Quebec would say, okay, we got 52 percent. Here is our interpretation of what we got. Here are the documents: sign on the dotted line.

"We'd start up immediately with the notion that if Canada was divisible, so was Quebec and that would have been a very interesting debate. Immediately. The Reform Party would have been important in the sense that they would have been taking a very hard line; they would have been pumping certain regions of the country."

Brian Tobin and his colleagues from the rest of Canada had entered the referendum campaign as doves. Most of them had supported the Meech Lake and Charlottetown attempts at constitutional reconciliation with Quebec. Some had political scars to show for their efforts. But facing the threat of a Yes vote, they felt that a more hawkish attitude was called for.

———

It should come as no surprise that by the end of the referendum campaign, the non-Quebec members of the federal cabinet were champing at the bit to take the lead in dealing with a Yes vote, or that some of them were contemplating putting Chrétien on a tight leash if it happened. One might be more inclined to ask why it took them so long to assert their place in a debate that had such profound implications for the voters who elected them. But then the Liberals on Parliament Hill had been told for months that there was no need to fret about the Quebec thing. It was a message they would faithfully take home to their ridings. It was only toward the end of the campaign that the upbeat official tone took on more sober undertones. Instead of all being well in the best of all worlds, the message shifted to the referendum being merely under control. As that happened, the largely blind trust that many ROC MPs and ministers had placed in Chrétien's Quebec inner circle declined precipitously.

Tobin, for one, was getting his own poll reports and not just the somewhat sanitized version that was regularly fed to the cabinet. By the last week of the campaign it was clear to the minister that actually very little was under control. "The numbers I received that week were from three different pollsters and I was talking to them directly so they were not getting paid for having a conversation. The No side was seven to fourteen points behind a week before the referendum."

Even from where he sat in Ottawa, physically separated from the Quebec scene by hundreds of kilometres and cut off from it by a language barrier that forced him to rely on mostly translated information, Tobin was convinced that the federalist camp was tone deaf. From his perspective, his side had no understanding of the root cause of Lucien Bouchard's impact on the campaign. "The federalists were not listening to what he was saying. He was a separatist. Separatists are bad. The guy has got horns on his head. But they were not listening to what he was saying. What he was saying was pretty brilliant.

"He was not saying anglophones in the rest of Canada are terrible people or bad people and we need to get away from them. What he was saying to Quebecers was they are actually nice people and they must be getting tired with us because we can't seem to make up our mind and it's really unfair to them and it is time to have a clear answer. We will be living side by side afterwards and we are going to figure out what the new relationship is, but you know the rest of Canada is so tired of this ongoing debate that it lost interest. They don't care. They just want us to be clear. And so let's be clear.

"That was a very powerful, very effective common sense argument to make to the average Quebecer who is not interested in the minutiae of the Constitution or NAFTA or the debt or who takes a share of it and how it is broken up. There are certain parts of the intelligentsia that want to know all these things; that want to know on the head of a pin how that gets sorted out. For the average guy who is a working person, who does not have the time or the apti-tude or the interest to delve into constitutional law, the notion of 'let's just be clear and then we will all be friends' was a powerful argument."

Brian Tobin was one of the key movers behind the

controversial pro-Canada rally that took place in Montreal on the last Friday of the campaign. He called up the head offices of corporate Canada to find money to finance it. He gave the officials who worked in his federal department a day off to encourage them to attend it.

Tobin says Lucien Bouchard's rhetoric that the rest of Canada no longer cared whether Quebec stayed or went inspired him to champion the initiative. But he acknowledges that while the rally provided an emotional outlet to many in the rest of Canada, it might also have hit a nerve in Quebec. "For people outside of Quebec it really is a powerful memory. They did it for themselves. So they could really say that they did not sit silent at such a time. It is probably not remembered the same way in Quebec. It is probably remembered in a very controversial way in Quebec.

"I don't know if I made a difference. It is my opinion that a very defeatist attitude set in among the federalist forces in Quebec and I think if it did nothing else it helped get the federalist vote out. But it might have encouraged sovereignists to also come out and vote."

Two decades after the referendum men and women who otherwise fought on the same side of the Quebec battle and who are equally committed to federalism still cannot come to anything approaching consensus on the merits of the October 27 pro-Canada rally. There will likely never be a reconciliation of their views.

But it is no longer terribly important to know whether the rally saved the federalist camp from an imminent defeat or whether it robbed it of a more definitive victory. In the larger scheme of federal political life, the fact that the rally took place at all has come to matter more than its debatable impact on the referendum vote.

The people who sat at Jean Chrétien's table did not realize it at the time but the pro-Canada rally marked the end of an era. Before it, the conception and implementation of Quebec/Canada policy was the virtual monopoly of politicians and strategists from that province.

New Brunswick senator Lowell Murray had overseen the ill-fated Meech Lake Accord as intergovernmental affairs minister under Brian Mulroney. And Joe Clark—a cabinet minister from Alberta—had led the negotiations that resulted in the dead-on-arrival Charlottetown Accord. But the intellectual energy behind the Meech Lake Accord came from the Quebec federalist government of Robert Bourassa. The premier and his lead minister on the file, Gil Rémillard, had lobbied the other provinces hard in preparation for the negotiations that led to the five-point deal. Nationally, Prime Minister Brian Mulroney, a Quebecer, was the driving force behind the accord. As for the Clark-led Charlottetown round, Quebec sat out most of it, leaving the federal government and the other provinces to put the yolk back in the egg that had been cracked over Meech Lake.

When Tobin suggested that thousands of non-Quebecers be brought into downtown Montreal to plead for Canada in the heated lead-up to the referendum vote, he hit a wall of

Quebec objections. Most of Chrétien's Quebec caucus, including lead referendum minister Lucienne Robillard, were vehemently opposed to the plan. Like the Quebec politicians who manned the No headquarters in Montreal, they believed that it was a reckless move that would backfire on the federalist camp. They stressed that the spending involved would break the Quebec referendum law and that news of that breach could cost precious votes. In more normal circumstances, history suggests that the Quebec caucus would have prevailed. The rule, after all, had always been that when it came to Quebec, Quebecers knew best.

But in this instance tradition flew out the window. According to Tobin it took less than half an hour for Chrétien to decide to override his Quebec ministers, give the rally his blessing and order his fisheries minister to make it happen. On this rarest of occasions, the ROC ministers had prevailed on a Quebec matter. For better and for worse it presaged the shape of things to come on Parliament Hill.

On the surface, the balance of power in cabinet and in the backrooms of the federal capital remained unchanged after the referendum. Jean Chrétien continued to govern—often successfully—for almost another decade. He won two more elections. And when he left, two more Liberal leaders from Quebec—Paul Martin and Stéphane Dion—replaced him in quick succession.

A victory, even if it is hard won and perilously close, is still a victory. After the referendum, Tobin and his fellow ministers from the rest of Canada did not bang on Chrétien's door and ask him to remove any Quebec ministers. The unity file continued to be managed by the Quebecers who sat in the PMO. And new recruits from Quebec such as Stéphane Dion and Pierre Pettigrew were parachuted into Liberal-friendly Montreal ridings before landing in high-profile cabinet roles designed to place them on the post-referendum front line.

The old ways of doing business with Quebec—honed over decades by successive Liberal and Progressive Conservative prime ministers—seemed to have secured a new lease on life.

But below the waterline the keel of the federal ship of state had shifted. The cabinet debate over the pro-Canada rally offered the first clues of an unstoppable movement. The ROC ministers who had elbowed their way to the Quebec table in the near panic of the last week of the referendum campaign did not leave the room after the episode. And their voices became leading ones in the debate over how to deal Quebec and with the unfinished business that resulted from the near-death referendum experience.

Tobin did not witness that evolution in person. After the referendum his relationship with Chrétien changed. So did his rapport with Lucien Bouchard. Within months of the Quebec vote, both he and the leader of the Bloc Québécois left Parliament Hill to become premiers of their respective provinces. It is over that period of his political career that Tobin got to know Bouchard as someone other than a fierce opponent.

It was an unlikely development that illustrates how politics does make for strange, or at least changing, bedfellows.

The first contact between the two men—when Bouchard was a Tory minister and Tobin an opposition critic—had not been auspicious. They'd had a spectacular clash at the tail end of the Meech Lake debate over the sustained opposition of Newfoundland's Liberal government to the constitutional accord. Bouchard had suggested from his seat on the government side of the House of Commons that it might be time for Canada to choose between Newfoundland and Quebec. He had made it sound as if the choice was a no-brainer. Tobin had been incensed. He says the two of them could have come to blows.

But in his new role as premier, Tobin got to know Lucien Bouchard better. He came to have a lot of time for his former foe. So did many of the other premiers, and in many instances the friendship was reciprocal. In fact, it is a poorly kept secret that Premier Bouchard ended up preferring the company of his fellow premiers to that of many of his fellow péquistes.

It is over their coincidental time as premiers that Tobin became convinced that Lucien Bouchard would not have let Jacques Parizeau seize a narrow Yes mandate to rush Quebec to independence. "I don't think that Jacques Parizeau was ever Lucien Bouchard's boss. The truth of the matter is that had there been a Yes vote, Mr. Parizeau would have been far less persuasive, broadly speaking, with Quebecers than Lucien Bouchard. In such circumstances, the power truly flows from the people of the province.

"It had always been my view that if the government of Quebec were to unilaterally declare independence, that would have been the best outcome for the federal government. Because it would have validated the federalist argument that this was not a mandate to negotiate a new arrangement. It was always about the sovereignists advancing their own argument about getting out of Canada.

"I think I know Lucien Bouchard well enough and that he has enough pride and enough sense of self that there would not have been the calculation that some might have made: Oh, we won, I'm on the winning team. I will go along with a UDI because l will share the glory of my new country. I think I know him well enough to know that if he felt betrayed, if he felt cut out of the loop, if he felt that he had been misled, he would not have been silent. I can't swear to that but I do not think that he would make the calculation that power comes first. He would make the calculation that integrity comes first.

"To want your own country is a very intoxicating thing. If you approach people who have a dream as if they were a bunch of evil people immediately, you are going to lose all ability to connect with them. But the dream cannot be based on a lie. If you ask a mandate for a partnership and you do a UDI, it's a lie. It's not something Bouchard would have done."

In 2000, Tobin returned to federal politics. He ran in that year's federal election, a move that fuelled speculation that a leadership bid was in the works. When he returned to Parliament, Chrétien's post-referendum strategy was already in place. At the request of the federal government in 1998, the Supreme Court had ruled extensively on matters pertaining to the issue of secession. A law (the Clarity Act) to spell out for the first time the terms on which Canada would engage on any future Quebec referendum had been drafted and passed with support from the Reform Party and the NDP two years later. Chrétien's post-referendum strategy had still been in its infancy when Tobin had left the federal cabinet. The notion that the government would pursue a dual track—Plan A dealing with the prime minister's commitment to constitutional and institutional reform, including the recognition of Quebec as a distinct society; and the more hardline Plan B designed to put a federal frame around future referendums—had not yet bloomed into actual legislation.

By the time Tobin returned, Plan A had wilted on the vine for lack of provincial and public support to engage on the Constitution and lack of federal Liberal appetite for a comprehensive devolution of powers to the provinces. Chrétien transferred the responsibility for job training to the premiers, and he passed a law that stipulated that Parliament would not ratify a constitutional amendment without the approval of Quebec, Ontario, Atlantic Canada, the Prairies and British Columbia. But those limited steps fell well short of the wholesale rebalancing of the federation and the constitutional reform that Quebec so badly desired. Plan B, on the other hand, had turned out to be overwhelmingly popular in the rest of Canada. It had attracted multi-party support in the House of Commons. In Quebec, Lucien Bouchard had tried and failed to whip up enough opposition to the Clarity Act to turn it into a springboard to another referendum. Instead, the act had provided the impetus for his mid-mandate resignation as premier and PQ leader.

Over his early years on the Hill, Tobin had been a Plan A type, a politician from the rest of Canada who had spent political capital on reconciliation with Quebec. But like the prospect of imminent death, the clear sight of a federalist defeat at the end of the 1995 referendum tunnel had changed his perspective. No longer did he want to be a mere passenger on a derailing train.

The Clarity Act was largely about re-empowering the rest of Canada in any future debates that arise over the shape of the federation. It was an outlet for the sense of exclusion felt by most non-Quebecers at the time of the referendum drama. And it was a clear expression of the more hard-nosed attitudes that resulted from discussions such as the one Tobin and his ROC colleagues held in the last week of the campaign to talk about *realpolitik* in a Canada without Quebec.

If Tobin had been around Chrétien's cabinet table to shape the post-referendum federal approach, he would have been among those ministers from outside Quebec who would have seen wisdom in taking a harder line. Memories of the federalist scare of the 1995 referendum may be fading, but its transformative impact on the mindset of the political class of the rest of Canada has endured.

CHAPTER 9

HUMPTY DUMPTY: PAUL MARTIN

In the bunker of the federal finance department, a powerless Paul Martin waited to see if the ticking time bomb of a Yes vote would blow up in Canada's face.

The finance minister's watch was not a lonely affair. Martin had an army of officials at his command. That night, all hands were on deck. "I think there were more people there that night than on a normal workday," he recalls. "But when the results started coming in you would have heard a pin drop. We were very nervous."

In the event of a Yes victory, this would be the first of many sleepless nights for Martin's team; the unenviable task of softening the blow of a federalist referendum defeat in the financial markets at home and abroad would be theirs.

Martin's initial mission was to buy Canada, its threatened loonie and its financial infrastructure some breathing room while the country's political leadership regrouped and figured out a way forward. Even if the minister succeeded in mitigating the initial market jitters that stood to hit the dollar and the banks—starting with the Quebec-based institutions—time would be of the essence. Canada would have to get its post-Yes act together swiftly.

It was a given that after a federalist defeat no one would believe it was business as usual in Canada. But the minister and his officials would have to make their most credible case that their government was stable and in control, even if in reality its world had just crashed.

To get a receptive hearing, Martin would first have to convince the Canada-savvy market watchers that Jean Chrétien as prime minister and he as finance minister were not by virtue of their Quebec political roots past their sell-by date. That stood to be a challenge.

If the result was a narrow Yes vote, he needed the market analysts and the financial commentators not to jump to the conclusion that Canada would break up or, short of that, that any reconfiguration of the country would at least be resolved in an orderly way. Pulling a convincing rabbit out of the thin air available in the country's unprepared capital would require the skills of a practiced political conjurer.

A bit more than a decade later, Paul Martin would lose the prime ministerial job after only two inconclusive years in Parliament Hill's corner office. Yet he says the pain of watching his hard-won grasp on power slip away in the 2006 election pales against the angst he felt on referendum night. "It was the longest night in my life—longer than the night I lost the election."

It was not just the federation as Canadians knew it—and as Martin sincerely loved it—that hung in the balance. For the minister of finance, the referendum vote was personal in more ways than just the patriotic one, and the stakes were as high as they were for the prime minister that he hoped to one day replace. Like Humpty Dumpty, Canada's most powerful minister was contemplating a great fall from a high Quebec wall; if it happened, it would be very hard to paste the broken pieces of his complex political persona together.

For one, a Yes vote stood to doom the ambitions of an aspiring prime minister who happened—as he did—to hold a seat in Quebec. Though an Ontarian by birth, Martin had put down deep roots in Montreal. The Quebec metropolis was his home and his political launch pad. When Martin had first run for elected office in 1988, that mix had looked like a recipe for leadership success.

Until recently the federal Liberals have tended traditionally to put a greater premium than other federal parties on a leadership candidate's appeal in Quebec. The province had been the key to their electoral success under Pierre Trudeau, and losing Quebec to Brian Mulroney in 1984 had turned their assumption that they owned Quebec on its head.

It is only since Jack Layton brought the province within the fold in 2011 that the New Democrats have put a high premium on the Quebec credentials of those who aspire to lead them. Conservative (and Progressive Conservative) interest in Quebec has tended to ebb and flow over the decades. The party's history has been marked by short, albeit intense, bursts of attention to Quebec and almost equally intense periods of disinterest.

In theory, after a Yes vote, Martin could have relocated to an Ontario seat. He still had strong ties to his native Windsor region; indeed, he chose that city to unveil his election platforms in 2004 and 2006. After the referendum, some of his followers discussed that possibility.

But in practice, in the event of a break-up of the federation he would always be one of the Quebec political figures on whose watch that seminal event had been set in motion. On that score, a Yes vote would find Martin and Chrétien at sea on the same leaky boat.

Paul Martin had spent his first five years in elected politics cooling his heels in opposition. He had been on the government side of Ottawa for only twenty-three months at the time of the Quebec vote and had barely started making his mark as finance minister. He had not yet acquired the patina of indispensability that restoring Canada to fiscal virtue would earn him over the coming years. If the referendum was lost, he risked being seen by many people as part of Canada's problem rather than part of its solution—starting with some of Martin's own cabinet colleagues. When Brian Tobin and other non-Quebec ministers had discussed the larger role they planned to take in a post-Yes federal cabinet, leaving the most crucial portfolio in the government to a minister from Quebec was not what they had in mind.

Paul Martin and Jean Chrétien had been leadership rivals. The peace between them was more in the nature of a truce and at times it was barely that. Their cooperation was uneasy, its terms defined by political necessity. In the climate of reciprocal suspicion between them, Martin had largely been kept out of Chrétien's referendum loop. And if the result had dictated that the prime minister rebalance his cabinet to make more room at the table for ROC ministers, he might not have been willing or able to go to the wall to keep Martin in finance.

While Martin expected Chrétien to resist the notion that a Yes vote should lead to his province's secession from Canada, and while Martin personally believed it should be resisted, he had no direct knowledge of the prime minister's intentions and no insights into the thinking of the other Quebecers in the cabinet or on the federalist front line in Quebec. "I did not know ministers who wanted to negotiate secession, but then I never discussed it with Lucienne Robillard or Jean Charest and never raised it in the conversations I had with Daniel Johnson."

Until the dying days of the referendum campaign, radio silence on the practical meaning of a Yes vote was par for the course among Canada's entire federalist political class (with the notable exception of the Reform Party). A former senior bureaucrat who followed the referendum campaign from behind the scenes of the federal capital notes that in the lead-up to the Quebec campaign, the mere hypothesis of a Yes vote was taboo, with its consequences discussed—in his words—only in whispers.

Late in the spring of 1995, when it had become certain that a fall referendum would be held in Quebec, Martin had ordered some measures be put in place to deal with potential referendum-induced disturbances on the markets and abroad. But they fell far short of an all-out contingency plan to soften the actual blow of a Yes vote.

For a number of years much of the Canadian debt had been financed on a short-term basis. That was cheaper in the long run, but it also meant that Canada had to refinance at least part of its debt every thirty, sixty or ninety days. A federalist referendum defeat would make that more expensive. Until the issue of Quebec's future was resolved, Canada would operate under a sword of Damocles—at the mercy of the markets after every up and down in what would be the most heated and possibly the most divisive existential debate in the country's history. In the aftermath of a federal loss, the longstanding Quebec/Canada differences stood to be compounded by political instability at the federal level and provincial divisions as to the way forward.

During his relatively short tenure as finance minister, Martin had taken steps to finance the debt over longer terms—a more pricey proposition that would pay off in the event of a Yes victory. But he notes that "it was not a quick process and we were still very vulnerable."

Even if the government had wanted or had been able to switch more of its debt over longer financing terms more quickly, its political messaging on the referendum would have made that difficult. The last thing Ottawa could afford was to signal that it might lose the referendum. Martin's step-by-step moves on the debt front had already raised eyebrows in the financial community: "Commentators would question our approach [because it was more expensive], but we could not go and tell them that it was because we feared the referendum. So we let them talk."

The collective mindset that prevented official Ottawa

from thinking through the immediate consequences of a Yes vote, and from preparing accordingly, persisted until the dying days of the referendum. Late that summer—with less than two months to go before the Quebec vote—a group of deputy ministers in the Chrétien government held retreats to discuss possible avenues for the second half of the Liberal mandate. I was invited to one of those discussions as a political commentator. One of the working assumptions of the brainstorming session I attended was that the unity issue would become dormant after the referendum and remain that way for a long time—possibly for the remainder of the professional lifespan of the people around the table. Much of the resources that had long been monopolized by the unity file would be transferred to other policy fronts. Of course, the opposite happened, with unity a larger federal concern after the referendum vote than in the period leading up to it.

Paul Martin himself had not had much time to get his head around the possibility of a Yes victory. As a Quebec minister he had spent much of the month of October on the campaign trail, and in the year leading up to the referendum his energies had been focused on the crafting of a landmark budget.

The budget that Paul Martin presented to the House of Commons in March 1995 was his second as finance minister but his first watershed one. It laid out a multi-year foundation for restoring the finances of the federal government and sent a loud and clear signal that Canada's government was determined to bite the fiscal bullet.

That marked a departure from the incremental approach to deficit reduction that the previous Tory government had implemented, without measurable success. Martin's deficit elimination strategy also went further than the plan that the Chrétien Liberals had sketched out in their 1993 campaign platform.

In politics the degree to which a government engages with a policy area ultimately matters as much as the substance of its policy. Little in the Liberal 1993 campaign Red Book—the policy document that had helped get Chrétien Liberals elected—had suggested that the new government would focus single-mindedly on the deficit. The party platform certainly did not herald deep cuts to social programs. And it actually promised to eliminate the GST, a commitment that turned out to be a mirage.

In a significant departure from the spirit of the Red Book, the 1995 budget made it clear that fiscal matters had the full attention of the ruling Liberals. In hindsight, that budget may have been the most positive collateral consequence of the complacency pervading Canada's capital in the year before the Quebec referendum.

"Honestly, the referendum did not loom large in our thinking when we prepared the 1995 budget," recalls its political author. "The background for it was international. We were thinking of the Mexico peso crisis and of looming financial disturbances in Asia. The referendum was not on the radar."

Had it dawned on the federal capital earlier that all might not turn up roses in the upcoming referendum, Paul Martin might have been forced to present a very different budget—one bearing only a vague resemblance to the decisive fiscal plan that put Canada on track for a string of ever-growing budget surpluses.

In government, one crisis chases off another. For all the resources at their disposal, modern governments are not particularly apt at walking and chewing gum at the same time. The hyper-centralization of power and decision-making around the prime minister is partly responsible for that. There is only so much that one individual and a small team of advisers can handle without dropping a few balls.

In the fall of 1994 and the winter of 1995, the Chrétien government had determined that the big hill it had to conquer was that of the deficit. It was crippling the government's capacity to acquit itself of its core social missions, let alone undertake the new ones that the Liberals were ideologically predisposed to dream about.

But if the prime minister and his strategists had believed that they would have the fight of their lives in Quebec come fall, had they imagined that the referendum would turn into the steep uphill climb that it did, they might have tooled down on the fiscal front. Taming the deficit might have had to wait for a time when the life of the government did not depend on its slaying a sovereignist dragon. When faced with a major threat, any government instinctively tries to reduce or eliminate the risk of complications on all the other fronts.

That would have been tragically ironic, for there is an after-the-fact consensus that even a year earlier Canada would have been much more vulnerable to the threat of a referendum defeat—when Martin's watershed budget was not yet in place. "In hindsight it was fortunate that we had the '95 budget," says the former minister. "Without it the mere prospect of a Yes victory would have hit the dollar."

Paul Martin spent the final weekend of the referendum campaign huddled with his officials, preparing for the worst-case scenario. His spring budget was the thread that held together the message he planned to deliver to the financial community in the event of a Yes vote.

"I would have said that Canada's economy was strong; that we had decisively addressed our deficit; that our last budget had been a huge success and that we were determined to stay the course. I would have said that if it came to separation, Canada would be strong enough to survive it; that it had natural resources, a solid economy, a deficit-elimination strategy—but that it was not a given that Quebec secession would result from the vote."

Much as Martin believed that negotiating Quebec secession was a non-starter, he also knew that a process of some sort would have to follow a Yes vote and that it would have to fall into place in short order. "Our biggest fear," he admits, "was uncertainty. The markets could not have accepted it."

No one expected Canada's international lenders to be patient in the face of chaos and dysfunction. Nor did the country's financial institutions, or for that matter the corporate leaders to whose ranks Martin had for many years belonged, have any appetite for moves that could have prolonged uncertainty resulting from a federalist defeat.

By October 30, 1995, the Bank of Canada and the country's financial institutions functioned on what one former senior official described as "an absolute assumption that there would be a negotiation and an orderly process moving forward."

For on Bay and Wall Streets, in the banking towers of corporate Canada and on the executive floors of the institutions that financed the country's debt, any attempt by the Chrétien government to stonewall Quebec's calls for talks based on a Yes victory and engage instead in a lengthy siege of the province's public opinion was considered a nightmare scenario.

There were precious few takers for a drawn-out battle to negate a Yes result if it meant having to do business in an uncertain climate on an open-ended basis. That was at least as true of Quebec's businesspeople as of those elsewhere in Canada. Like their counterparts across the country, some of the federalist champions in the province's business establishment would have preferred any resolution between the two governments to a trench war—a fight that even still might not keep the federation whole.

At a meeting the Business Council on National Issues (BCNI)—the country's most influential corporate lobby group—held shortly after the referendum, in the days when a rematch seemed inevitable, the notion of proactively coming out in favour of separate national arrangements for Quebec and Canada was raised. The idea was to pre-empt another referendum and the havoc of a possible federalist defeat by fast-forwarding to a new normal. Those discussions did not lead to a change in the pro-federalist tack of the BCNI, but they do reveal the mindset of part of corporate Canada as it contemplated the uncertainty that would have resulted from a sovereignist vote in Quebec. For many of its members a quick peace—even at the cost of a broken-up federation—would have been preferable to a drawn-out war to keep Quebec in Canada.

The finance minister's own Plan A for a Yes victory would have been "negotiations that did not lead to secession." As it happens that would also have been the only approach that would have secured a front-row seat at the table for any minister from Quebec. But it is unclear how Paul Martin and the federal government would have enticed Quebec's sovereignist leadership to show up for talks if Jacques Parizeau's core objective was off the table before the discussion had even started.

Moreover, as the situation deteriorated for the federalist camp during the referendum campaign, Martin and others in the federal government had actually spent more time working out a response to a potential UDI than giving consideration to a process that could channel a Yes mandate into a softer more federation-friendly outcome.

After the referendum, as the ROC ministers became more engaged in the Quebec issue, Paul Martin instead distanced himself from the file.

His strained relationship with Jean Chrétien had something to do with that distance; in time the lack of trust between the two leading Quebecers in the government festered into a Liberal civil war and, shortly after his re-election at the head of a third consecutive majority government, into an attempt to force Chrétien out of office.

But some of Martin's former Quebec colleagues feel that there was also an element of political calculation in his disengagement from the post-referendum debate, and they provide examples to back up their suggestion that he set himself apart from them on the issue for reasons other than just his simmering conflict with the prime minister. Soon after the referendum Jean Chrétien set up a federal scholarship program to mark the coming millennium. Quebec's political class was virtually unanimous in denouncing the initiative as a federal intrusion in the province's affairs. The Constitution stipulates that education is an exclusive provincial responsibility.

From Stéphane Dion to Pierre Pettigrew and Lucienne Robillard, the federal ministers from Quebec declined to defend the initiative. None of them had been consulted beforehand. Chrétien's wishes went straight into Paul Martin's annual budget, and the rest of the cabinet only found out about the program shortly before the finance minister announced it in the House of Commons. The other Quebec ministers were taken aback by Martin's quiet acquiescence to Chrétien's wishes.

The introduction of the Clarity Act prompted many heated debates around the cabinet table. Many of those pitted Quebec ministers against their ROC colleagues. Some of Martin's former Quebec colleagues privately complained that they had found him to be less than engaged in those discussions. At the time one of his otherwise loyal supporters in the Quebec cabinet told me that, even in private, he had found Martin to be less than forthcoming on the issue. He compared getting a handle on the finance minister's thinking on the Clarity Act to trying to hold a slippery fish with bare hands.

Paul Martin and his team were conducting a full-press courtship of the parliamentary media over that period, but the finance minister largely kept his thoughts about Quebec to himself. He so successfully disassociated himself from the file that five years later a young Liberal activist from Winnipeg would describe justice minister Martin Cauchon to me as Quebec's most important minister.

It could be that the near-death experience of the referendum convinced Paul Martin that the wooing of Quebec nationalists was not his strong suit. He had been burnt over the second half of the 1995 campaign when he had predicted that a Yes vote would impact a million jobs. The figure stuck, but not in the way the minister might have hoped. Within hours of making that Quebec speech Martin was being attacked from all corners of Quebec—including some usually friendly ones—for fear mongering. His frantic calls to his most amicable Quebec media contacts, and there was no lack of those, had failed to yield more lenient analyses of his comments.

When the scandal over the management of the sponsorship program broke immediately after Jean Chrétien's retirement, Paul Martin could truthfully swear that he had had nothing to do with the initiative. That was also the finding of the public inquiry that Quebec justice John Gomery conducted on the sponsorship matter. But Martin's efforts to insulate himself from the post-referendum handling of the Quebec file could not insulate the province's most visible minister from the collective responsibility attached to the ethical derailment of a unity-driven program.

After he became prime minister, Paul Martin negotiated an asymmetrical health accord with the provinces that respected Quebec's longstanding resolve to keep the federal government out of the policy areas that fall under the exclusive constitutional responsibility of the provinces. But the solid connection that he had once sought with the province's francophone voters eluded him. Driven away by the scandal that resulted from the abuse of the federal sponsorship program, thousands of Quebec federalist voters stayed home rather than vote for the Martin Liberals (or for the

Bloc Québécois) in 2004. Many returned in 2006, only to cast their vote for Stephen Harper's Conservative Party, leaving the post-Chrétien, post-Martin Liberals on the outside looking in.

CHAPTER 10

A HANGING IN THE MORNING:
RAYMOND CHRÉTIEN

By all indications Canadian ambassador Raymond Chrétien was only a few hours away from his fifteen minutes of American network fame. The prospect was as sobering as a hanging in the morning.

For the early hours of the day after the vote, the schedule of Canada's envoy to Washington read more like that of a rock star on a promotional tour than that of a career diplomat. Tantalized by the news potential of a Yes victory, the American networks had eagerly booked the ambassador for their breakfast shows. His agenda was packed tight with television hits.

The fact that Chrétien was the nephew of the Canadian prime minister—who stood to be thrown under the bus after a federalist referendum defeat—made the ambassador an even juicier catch. By virtue of his strong links to the prime minister, Raymond Chrétien would be closer to the eye of a post-Yes storm than many of the politicians who were physically in Canada. In the event of a disaster on the scale of a federalist loss, he would serve the dual role of informed eyewitness and aggrieved next-of-kin. For broadcast news, it was an ideal combination.

Getting Canada on the overcrowded Washington radar is usually a diplomatic challenge. At the best of times the U.S. media have little appetite for political news involving America's northern neighbour. The word *short* does not begin to capture the brevity of its attention span for Canadian stories. But in this instance, the American media were on a binge. Their audience could not get enough of the Quebec referendum story.

"I don't think that there ever was an issue in the history of Canada/U.S. relations that got the attention of the American public like the referendum did," recalls Chrétien. "People would stop me on the street to talk about the referendum! I spent seven years in the United States and even during the Turbot War [involving overfishing off the east coast], even during the debate on the Iraq War I never had a day like the day of the referendum.

"To see CNN report the Quebec results every fifteen minutes was unprecedented. None of my predecessors and none of my successors was ever under the American microscope in this fashion. It was the most delicate file I had to handle."

That unusual amount of American interest was confirmation that the federalist No camp was in deep trouble. In Canada, political correctness often prevented pundits from acknowledging that the referendum could be lost to the sovereignist side. No shortage of partisan spin doctors stormed the sets of domestic news shows to argue that those who raised the spectre of a federalist defeat were out of their depth. If the referendum doomsayers happened to be francophones, it was sometimes suggested—for good measure—that they were allowing themselves to be blinded by a pro-sovereignty bias.

In some instances the offenders—if they hailed from the business community—might get a call from high up in the government to remind them that to wax publicly about a possible sovereignist victory, to offer speculation as to its aftermath, stood to sap federalist morale and hurt the greater cause of Canada. But if federalist forces could prevent the business community from talking about it, they couldn't stop it from thinking through its options.

Rather than depend exclusively on government sources to keep track of the situation in Quebec, a number of Canadian financial institutions had secured independent analyses of their own as early as 1994, at the time of the provincial election that brought Jacques Parizeau to power. The PQ was no more enamoured of such initiatives than its federalist rivals. Both sides had little patience with anyone interfering with their control of their respective messages.

On one occasion during the 1994 Quebec election campaign, Jacques Parizeau had had one of his leading economic recruits call a Toronto-based financial institution to suggest in less-than-subtle terms that it should cease and desist from contracting out for independent assessments of the Quebec political scene if it wanted to do business with the incoming Parti Québécois government.

But in Washington, the financial analysts—the people from the bond ratings agencies whom Chrétien polled frequently for insight—had no qualms about ruffling Canadian government feathers in the federal capital. They delivered unvarnished assessments of the evolving Quebec situation and the ambassador recalls that the picture they painted was grim for the federalists. "Over the last weeks of the campaign, I would talk to people who had their finger on the pulse of the campaign daily and to a man and woman they believed the Yes could win."

Given that Raymond Chrétien was sitting in the U.S., somewhat removed from the Quebec campaign trail and its feuding clans, one might assume that what he was hearing from his American sources would be old news in the federal capital. There was, after all, an army of government officials whose sole job it was to oversee the referendum and examine all its angles. Moreover, the scores of federal politicians who were campaigning in the province would normally be expected to have their ear to the ground and report on what they heard.

In fact, and rather alarmingly from the ambassador's point of view, the intelligence he gathered in New York and Washington often put him ahead of the Ottawa curve. Some of his federal contacts were hearing similarly pessimistic assessments of the federalist campaign; others had a gut feeling that things were going downhill fast for the No side. But reality was slow to jell in the backrooms of Parliament Hill and even slower to translate into effective action.

"Based on what I was hearing in the financial community

I was one of those who gave Ottawa a wake-up call. After such meetings I would hit the phone. The message was more credible from the federal perspective because it came from non-partisan sources, from sources that were mostly favourable to the survival of the Canadian federation. The financial analysts did not like what they saw but they called it as they saw it."

The gap Raymond Chrétien regularly found between his read of the Quebec situation and prevailing wisdom in official Ottawa was particularly wide when it came to assessing Bouchard's ascendance within the Yes campaign. "There are people [in the federal government] who took a while to realize the impact of the recasting of Lucien Bouchard as the lead Yes campaigner. Some in Ottawa did not see that coming and when it did they did not fully measure it for a while," recalls Chrétien.

"The moment I saw Bouchard take over, I thought that for us things would go downhill from there, that it would all become a lot more difficult. He was like the Holy Ghost, people wanted to touch him. How were we supposed to fight against that?"

In politics, the path well travelled is usually the one taken. To tinker with or even to question a strategy or an approach that has worked in the past is not readily done.

"For many in the federal government, the 1980 referendum was the template for the 1995 campaign. They had fought the previous campaign. They took victory for granted. That's why there was no fallback plan."

From Washington, Raymond Chrétien enjoyed a bird's-eye view of the Quebec scene and had easy access to top-notch referendum analysis. But his insights also stemmed from a unique set of personal connections.

The 1995 Yes and No camps were riddled with dysfunctional relationships. On a good day, Jean Chrétien and Daniel Johnson had little to say to each other. As much as possible, the Quebec Liberal leader wanted the prime minister out of his hair. No one really talked to Lucienne Robillard. Jean Charest, as leader of a rival party to the ruling Liberals, was naturally suspicious of the motivations of the prime minister and his team, and vice versa. By referendum night the prospect of a Yes vote was pulling the Quebec federal ministers and their colleagues from the rest of Canada in different directions. Their political interests in the event of a federalist defeat dictated different courses. If not a divorce at least a trial separation was on several minds.

Over on the sovereignist side Parizeau, Bouchard and Dumont were hard-pressed to spend time together in the same room—to wit, Bouchard and Dumont's fortuitous decision to bail out of the referendum-night Yes rally before Parizeau had spoken. The premier's former aide, Jean Royer, notes that "rarely have people as different as Jacques Parizeau and Lucien Bouchard worked together on the same objective without going for each other's throat." (Author's note: they might have after a Yes vote.)

In contrast, Raymond Chrétien was not only close to

the prime minister, he was also a friend of the leader of the Bloc Québécois. A taxing privilege during the referendum, his family links to Jean Chrétien and his friendship with Lucien Bouchard gave the ambassador a degree of access to the two main federal protagonists enjoyed by no one else.

Lucien Bouchard had been a law school classmate and a foreign affairs colleague during his days as Brian Mulroney's ambassador to France. Even in his latest position as leader of the sovereignist Bloc Québécois he proved an occasional ally. At the time of Raymond Chrétien's appointment to Washington in 1994, Bouchard had come through for his friend.

In Canada's diplomatic pecking order, the Washington embassy is at the top of the list. Raymond Chrétien was a veteran diplomat who had served in senior foreign affairs positions in Ottawa and in a string of foreign capitals. But given the prime minister's family tie to his proposed Washington envoy, the appointment raised a few eyebrows in the Canadian capital.

Though leader of the opposition, Bouchard put an end to the discussion. Recalls the former ambassador, "He said: 'I will never get to appoint a Canadian envoy to Washington, but if I did I would send Raymond Chrétien.' It was very helpful."

After Chrétien's transfer to the U.S. capital, the two had cooperated behind the scenes on a number of files—notably the softwood lumber dispute that pitted the American industry against its Canadian competition. "I knew that if I phoned Lucien he would take my call quickly, because in

Washington I was in a strategic position for both federalists and sovereignists. Also he knew that I was in the loop of a lot of things on Parliament Hill. We kept the channels open. Sometimes talking directly can help avert some pretty damaging situations."

It is fair to say that Bouchard trusted Raymond Chrétien far more than he trusted Jacques Parizeau. It is even possible that at some point the Bloc leader tried to persuade his former classmate to join him on the Yes barricades or that he encouraged others to try to win him over.

Parsing the former ambassador's careful words makes apparent that the option of switching sides was put to him, directly or indirectly. "People would tell me: if you left your post in Washington to join the Yes side, it would be game over for federalism. There were people who thought like that, who sought that before the referendum. That was how it was back then."

But Chrétien was tied to the federalist side by more than just love for Canada. He was closer to the prime minister than anyone in the federal cabinet. While ministers such as Paul Martin or Lucienne Robillard talked to Jean Chrétien through his advisers, his nephew only had to pick up the phone to speak with his uncle directly. On issues pertaining to the state of the referendum campaign, he did so frequently. "Sometimes," he recalls, "we used Quebec slang to throw off any eavesdroppers."

But Raymond Chrétien was of course more than a dutiful nephew who occasionally acted as a sounding board to a somewhat doting uncle. He was also performing high-level referendum-related diplomatic work. And on that score, the fact that he was known to have the ear of the prime minister made some Washington doors easier to open than if he had just been a distinguished foreign affairs careerist.

Some of his work paid off in the last week of the campaign when President Bill Clinton publicly professed his preference for a united Canada. Clinton was very popular in Quebec and some analysts credit his intervention for having moved a few percentage points of support back to the No camp. At a minimum it helped the federalist camp sustain the late momentum it so desperately needed.

The prime minister had a solid relationship with President Clinton but it was Raymond Chrétien who ensured that there was no distortion and little outside interference on the Washington/Ottawa line. "By the end of the campaign I was constantly liaising with the White House. President Bill Clinton and his entourage had the lead on the file, not the State Department. Every statement from the U.S. administration was worked out in close consultation with the embassy. So we had no surprises. They wanted to be helpful. The Americans never flirted with ambiguity with the issue in the way that France did. For them the objective was to help the Canadian federation and its government."

There is little doubt that if Canada and Quebec had agreed to some degree of separation, the United States would have accommodated it. But not without disruptions. NAFTA—the agreement that governed trade between Canada, the U.S. and Mexico—would have needed to be adjusted to include a fourth government partner. A different place for Quebec in the North American geopolitical space would have had to be carved out. And there was no guarantee that the other provinces would necessarily soldier on together as Canada minus Quebec.

Given a choice between a stable geopolitical status quo and the uncertainty of a process aiming to substantially reconfigure its Canadian partner, the White House was dealing with a no-brainer.

Beyond the U.S., the possible break-up of the Canadian federation was also worrisome for the chain reaction that it might set off in other parts of the world. The fall of the Berlin Wall in 1989 and the subsequent decline of the Soviet empire had ignited nationalist powder kegs in a number of former Eastern Bloc countries—most notably Yugoslavia. There was little appetite in Washington and abroad for the advent of even more new nation-states carved out of existing ones.

American public opinion was also less sympathetic to the Quebec sovereignty movement than was its French counterpart, and not just because of the absence of a common language. "In the U.S., the sovereignty movement tries to cast its project as Quebec's war for independence, but many Americans see it more as a variation on their civil war and that makes it unappealing to many of them," notes Raymond Chrétien.

Based on his contacts with the White House, Ambassador Chrétien expected President Clinton's support of the federal government to remain unflagging in the aftermath of a Yes victory. In politics, nothing is eternal, and in time

Washington, like corporate Canada, would likely have pressed for an orderly resolution rather than tolerate an open-ended period of chaotic uncertainty on its northern border. Still, in the first difficult days after a Yes vote, the Canadian government need not have feared that the Americans would try to force its hand by falling in step with the secessionist parade. It could also hope that the Clinton White House would bring its influence to bear on the international community to do the same and to at least stick to a wait-and-see attitude for Quebec and Canada.

"If the Yes had won, the first twenty-four to forty-eight hours would have been really difficult. In the case of a Yes, not every one of our foreign allies would have necessarily had the same take as we did but the Americans had told us they would back us, whatever our decision."

As the results rolled in on October 30, Raymond Chrétien remained confident he could count on the White House reaction to a federalist defeat. But he says he was less certain of the marching orders he would be issued from Ottawa prior to his hitting the morning television circuit. He would not officially get those until the outcome of the vote was known.

He may have had a heads-up from Jean Chrétien as to the prime minister's intentions in the event of a federalist defeat. They talked so frequently that it would certainly have come up. But if he did get advance notice of Chrétien's leanings, it was given in confidence—from uncle to nephew, not from prime minister to ambassador—and so it remains.

What is certain is that if the Yes had won, Raymond Chrétien would have been one of the first to know what the prime minister was going to say and do about it, likely before most of the government's senior ministers.

"I was in constant contact with the prime minister that evening. And there was certainly a plan in the heads of people like Jean Pelletier [Liberal chief of staff] and Jean Chrétien. They would have turned around quickly, during the night. I was expected to be on deck at six a.m. I would have had talking points and a message by then. It was a coherent government and it functioned efficiently."

There has never been a relationship between a sitting prime minister and the country's lead ambassador like that of Jean and Raymond Chrétien. It is unlikely ever to be replicated. The fact that Raymond Chrétien was to have been Canada's face on the American networks the morning after a Yes vote is a token of the extraordinary margin of manoeuvre that he enjoyed.

Of all the people interviewed for this book, he had a unique perspective. His position as a front-line Canadian diplomat at a time of great domestic tension was of course unlike that of any of the other players, as were his close personal connections to both Jean Chrétien and Lucien Bouchard. That combination probably explains why his take on the aftermath of a Yes vote is the most surgical of any of the Quebecers we interviewed.

Paul Martin argued that being from the province made him and his Quebec colleagues somehow more valuable.

His rationale was that it would be easier for Quebec federalist politicians to stand up to a Yes vote than for elected officials from other regions of the country. Raymond Chrétien was more inclined to cut to the chase.

"The political future of all the Quebecers associated with the federal government, people like André Ouellet and Jean Chrétien, would have been in question. And if the legitimacy of the government had taken a hit, so would my own legitimacy since I was a federal appointee. In my case it would have been even more flagrant as my last name was Chrétien."

He also acknowledges that arriving at a post-Yes consensus within the ranks of the Liberal government itself would have been a challenge: "Some ministers might have called for Jean Chrétien to go; others might have resigned. Some would have called for a federal referendum to test the result of the Quebec one. Jean Chrétien, for his part, would not have accepted a weak Yes."

And what of his friend Lucien Bouchard? From where Raymond Chrétien sat, in the event of a Yes victory the way forward for the sovereignists would not have been any more tidily laid out than that of the defeated federal government: "Bouchard knew Ottawa. That is an asset few Quebecers have. But what would he have wanted? Sovereignty-association? We knew where Parizeau stood but it was less clear in Bouchard's case. I always thought that he might not seek the same thing as Parizeau, but what it was that he was seeking, I don't know. I suspect he did not know either."

In the end, Ambassador Chrétien had little need for the talking points that eventually came from Ottawa on referendum night. Minutes after the federalist victory was declared, half of his television appearances were cancelled. And on those programs that still wanted him, it was a lot easier to talk up a victory—even one as narrow as that—than it would have been to buy time for the federalist side scrambling to regain its footing.

But perhaps more importantly, the networks that did interview Raymond Chrétien the morning after the referendum were not terribly interested in how close the result had been. "From the American perspective, it did not matter whether the No had won with one half of one percent or with 25 percent. It was done, period," recalls Chrétien. "For me that was very revealing. The U.S. is a superpower. A Yes vote could have brought some slight changes to the North American dynamics. But it did not happen. That was the end of the story."

It would take a few more years, but eventually Canada would come to pretty much the same conclusion.

CHAPTER 11

THE ACCIDENTAL TOURIST: ANDRÉ OUELLET

I n the hours after a Yes victory, Jean Chrétien's Quebec lieutenant would have wanted his government to jump from the frying pan of the lost referendum into the fire of a repeat vote held under federal auspices.

Left to his own devices, André Ouellet, foreign affairs minister and the prime minister's second-in-command in Quebec, would have conveyed the imminence of a second Quebec referendum to the United States and France, the two foreign powers whose reaction to either result stood most to set the tone for the international community. "I would have told the American administration that we would ask Quebecers to answer a clearer question; that we would put to them the stark question of whether they wanted to separate from Canada and have their own country or stay in the federation.

"I would have told France that with that close a result on an ambiguous question it should not rush to recognize Quebec's independence until we had had Quebecers revisit their vote and answer the more straightforward question of whether they wanted to stay or go."

Ouellet's comments are true to form. It was always his political style to rush where angels (sometimes wisely) feared to tread. His street-fighting instincts were second to none, except perhaps Jean Chrétien himself.

That being said, he is careful to point out that the idea of a federally initiated repeat referendum was never discussed in cabinet. In the same breath Ouellet readily admits that— like the other senior ministers in the Liberal government and in spite of his specific political responsibilities in Quebec—he had received no word of Chrétien's plans for a Yes vote. "We never debated post-defeat scenarios at the cabinet table. We did not even get regular poll numbers. On that basis it is just my personal opinion that we would have held our own referendum. But I was convinced that we would never accept a Quebec Yes. I never thought the [1995] referendum would settle the issue one way or another."

There was a time when Ouellet had a finger in every Quebec political pie. During the late seventies and early eighties, the Liberal MP for Papineau had been Prime Minister Pierre Trudeau's chief Quebec organizer and his lead fixer in the province.

Over that period he had held half a dozen mid-level ministerial briefs, such as minister of Canada Post, public works and labour. In those days his influence was larger than his second-tier cabinet titles suggested.

But by the 1995 referendum that career momentum was waning and political retirement was on the horizon. Ouellet had started to step back from the Quebec fray. He had spent the Liberal Party's opposition years in the constitutional trenches, participating in the many parliamentary committees that had toured the country to discuss the issue with Canadians. He had represented the Liberal Party on Quebec's post-Meech Bélanger-Campeau Commission. He was no longer so eager to collect bruises on behalf of his party in hand-to-hand combat with sovereignist foes. Some of them—starting with Lucien Bouchard, whom he had first met in university—were his friends. He and Chrétien, on the other hand, were personally not that close.

As minister of foreign affairs, Ouellet sat on the front row of the cabinet in a role more senior than any other Quebec minister, with the exception of Paul Martin. But it was a position that kept him out of the House of Commons, the federal capital and the country during extended trips abroad. By definition, his ministerial role prevented him from engaging in many of the heated debates about the government's domestic agenda.

It is not rare for the foreign affairs minister in any government to become a bit of a tourist in Parliament and at the cabinet table. But it is quite rare for a prime minister to choose a jet-setting minister to be his political lieutenant in a province gearing up for a vote as crucial as the Quebec referendum.

The 1995 federal Liberal organization that Ouellet was nominally responsible for overseeing was the rusty shell of the formerly well-oiled machine that used to deliver Quebec to the party throughout the Trudeau years. In the 1993 election, Liberals had won less than one-third of the province's seats. They'd had to fight hard just to ensure that Jean

Chrétien reclaim his former seat of Saint-Maurice. The riding had swung to the Tories after he quit politics for the private sector in 1986. With Progressive Conservative support in full meltdown, the Bloc Québécois had dearly hoped to deprive Canada's incoming prime minister of a seat in the Commons.

It had been a close enough call that one well-respected pollster actually forecast the Liberal leader's defeat. At his first news conference as prime minister, Chrétien proudly waved the local front-page prediction of his loss before the television cameras.

In spite of ominous creaks in the Liberal machine and notwithstanding his title as Quebec lieutenant, Ouellet was, if not an absentee mechanic, at least a distracted one. His ministerial schedule simply did not leave a lot of time for behind-the-scenes partisan work. Moreover, his public contribution to the Quebec debate came with serious elec-toral limitations. By his own admission, the veteran minis-ter was almost as radioactive in Quebec nationalist circles as his leader.

Ouellet's years as Liberal chief organizer in the mid-seventies had coincided with the rise of the Parti Québécois and the advent of a first sovereignist government in Quebec City. Over that period the federal minister had engaged in count-less verbal brawls with the péquistes. He ruffled feathers not only within the sovereignty movement but also within the ranks of the province's soft nationalists, the swing voters who stood to make a difference between a Yes and a No on referendum day.

Given his poor standing in his home province, Ouellet had heavily promoted the idea that someone with Lucienne Robillard's more nationalist-friendly profile be named as the federal government's go-between with Quebec's provincial Liberals. He had hoped her presence would help keep the channels open between capitals. Although Robillard's mission failed, Ouellet does not believe he would have done better himself. On the contrary, he feels he would have had an even harder time staking out some useful ground. "My relationship with Quebecers was not great. I had spent my career feuding with the PQ. I acted on many voters like a red flag to a bull."

That is actually an understatement. In 1984 the Progressive Conservatives had turned Ouellet into a lightning rod for Quebecers' fatigue with the federal Liberals. Over his first election campaign Brian Mulroney rarely delivered a speech in Quebec without mercilessly portraying André Ouellet as the poster boy for Liberal abuse of the province. It almost always struck a chord with the audience.

Ouellet was offside not only with the Quebec chattering class and the soft nationalists. First, he had supported John Turner against Jean Chrétien when the two had competed to succeed Pierre Trudeau in 1984. Compounding the injury six years later, Ouellet had been a vocal supporter of the Meech Lake Constitutional Accord at the time when Chrétien was riding the anti-Meech Liberal tide to the leadership. In opposition, Ouellet had stepped on more than his share of Liberal caucus toes over the constitutional issue. But after their successful 1993 election campaign, Chrétien and his brain trust were fully aware of the poor shape of the party's organization in Quebec. Still, they were disinclined to see the battle-weary Ouellet as an indispensable part of its recovery.

His paradoxical appointment as Quebec lieutenant and minister of foreign affairs was largely designed to keep control of the Quebec political file in the hands of one Jean Pelletier, Chrétien's chief of staff. He and the prime minister were old friends and former classmates. Chrétien would have trusted Pelletier with his life—something he would never say about Ouellet.

Even in his grand role as minister of foreign affairs, Ouellet was destined in the event of a Yes win to play second fiddle—to the prime minister's well-connected nephew in Washington and to Jean Pelletier's back-door approaches to France. The latter had gotten to know French president Jacques Chirac when they had been mayors of Quebec City and Paris, respectively, in the late seventies and eighties. Persuading the French government to hold its pro-sovereignty fire after a Yes vote would have been Pelletier's primary mission.

Ouellet acknowledges that his referendum role on the diplomatic front was mostly a supporting one. "I had done [an international] tour to spread the message that we would win. You can't show up in a foreign capital saying that you will lose." Still, at every stop along the way he had urged his foreign vis-à-vis to avoid jumping to conclusions no matter how the referendum turned out. Based on his travels, his impression was that Ottawa would have to take the initiative quickly if it wanted to stem a pro-Quebec movement, in particular within La Francophonie, the international association of francophone countries.

"I thought that a few African countries might jump the gun and support Quebec's independence bid. The Quebec government had done a lot of advance work in Africa. La Francophonie had a number of pro-independence members. It is possible that some of them would have lined up behind Quebec quickly."

If the Yes had won, Ouellet would have received marching orders from the PMO in much the same way as Ambassador Raymond Chrétien. But given that the diplomat was in more direct contact with the prime minister than Ouellet, chances are that Raymond Chrétien would have had more input in the crafting of those orders than the minister to whom he officially reported.

Both behind the scenes and on stage, Ouellet's referendum contribution ultimately amounted to a lot less than what would normally be expected of the prime minister's regional lieutenant during a crisis. But it was a deficit for which he would more than make up a few months after the vote.

Although Ouellet knew he carried too much baggage in Quebec to ever be a star on the No camp speaking circuit, he noticed during his limited campaigning that Tory leader Jean Charest had become the federalists' major attraction. Shortly after the referendum, Ouellet would leave politics to become the head of Canada Post; but, just before departing the scene, he went rogue on Jean Chrétien. In a year-end interview that set the cats among the Quebec Liberal pigeons, he suggested that opposition leader Daniel Johnson should bow out in favour of Jean Charest. When published, Ouellet's comments caused a furor in Ottawa and Quebec City. Charest scrambled to distance himself from the suggestion, as did Chrétien and his advisers. But the seed had been planted and barely two years later Charest would take the reins of the Quebec Liberals.

A final note: We met André Ouellet at his Alta Vista house in Ottawa. Like Jean Chrétien he has chosen to retire in Ontario rather than head back to Quebec. These days his forays in his native province are those of a visitor.

Given his track record, there is no doubt that Ouellet will go to his grave with the well-earned reputation of die-hard federalist. Over the course of our interview he spoke at length about his feeling that the Liberal government had missed an opportunity when it declined to set a referendum threshold in the Clarity Act (he was no longer at the cabinet). Ouellet says that the federal law should have spelled out, black and white, that the government of Canada would not consider that Quebec had a mandate to negotiate secession unless it met a higher referendum threshold than that of a simple 50-plus-1 majority.

And yet this retired federalist warrior sounds almost

wistful when he talks about Quebec sovereignty and his friend Bouchard's referendum performance. "As I see it, Lucien Bouchard had the same idea as René Lévesque. One does not bring a people to the brink of an abyss to then say: we are all in the hole together. The path to sovereignty is a long road that involves taking control of one's destiny, one's economy one step at a time. The fruit has to be allowed to ripen before it is picked. There is nothing bad in that . . ."

CHAPTER 12

THE DIVORCE COUNSELLOR: PRESTON MANNING

P reston Manning did not have a speech ready for referendum night. In the event of a federalist defeat, the
Reform Party leader knew exactly what he would tell
the prime minister. "I expected him to resign on that night
or shortly thereafter."

Manning was not just after Jean Chrétien. He would not
have been content with a reshuffling of the cabinet deck as
some Liberal ministers from the rest of Canada had in mind.
He was not ready to support or join any sort of coalition
government that would still be led by the Liberals. The
Reform leader wanted the entire government to resign.

In the likely scenario that the Liberals and their leader
did not comply, he was prepared to do whatever it took to
shut down Parliament or, short of that, render it impotent
and force an election. As a first step, Manning says he would
have made speeches so fiery that they "would have peeled
the paint off the ceiling of the House of Commons. Chrétien
would not have had weeks or months. You can just imagine
the speeches that would have been made about his role in all

this. In fact, I used to make them afterwards, telling him that as prime minister he came the closest to losing the federation. It is hard to forget that.

"I would have told the Liberals: you were entrusted, for better and for worse, with the future of the federation. You have failed and you are the last people that can negotiate with this bunch that has just won the referendum. Western Canada will not recognize your legitimacy."

If verbal missiles in the House failed to sink the Liberal government, Manning was ready to go further: "You would have had Western members leave Parliament and not come back because it would have been considered illegitimate." He says the voters who had elected fifty-two Reform members to the House of Commons two years before would have expected no less from his party. "The West in particular would not have trusted anyone in that government to handle the negotiations. They would have been scared stiff of what they'd sell off. The Liberals had paid no attention to the West in the whole process running up to the result. Why would they all of sudden represent its interests?"

The Reform threat to undermine the already depleted moral authority of a post-Yes federal government was not an empty one. With fifty-two MPs the Reform Party had finished the 1993 election only two seats behind the Bloc Québécois—to put that in context, even combined the Tories and the New Democrats didn't have enough members to warrant official party status in the House.

Jean Charest, a Quebecer whose riding had voted yes, led

the decimated Tories, and the NDP's Alexa McDonough was a rookie leader. The New Democrats had held a leadership vote a few weeks before the referendum, and McDonough— who had until then been a member of the Nova Scotia legislature—had yet to win a seat in Parliament. To all intents and purposes, Manning was the leader of the federalist opposition in the House of Commons.

Manning's party held only one seat east of Manitoba. It was glaringly absent from Atlantic Canada. The Reform leader was convinced, however, that his party's fortunes would change in the aftermath of a Yes vote. "I think a party like mine, which would have taken a very hard line that this is an election whose sole purpose is to elect a government that represents the interest of the rest of the country, would have earned a mandate. We would have said we're no longer in the business of accommodating, that we are in the business of protecting our own interests."

In the latter stages of the referendum campaign, Jacques Parizeau had sent emissaries to feel out the Reform Party in the aftermath of a Yes vote. They had told Manning's advisers that they anticipated a 52 percent victory. They had asked the Reform entourage what its boss would make of a result in that range. According to Jean Royer, the Quebec premier's chief of staff, the answer had been encouraging. Upon a Yes victory, Parizeau could expect the Reform leader to call for talks to set the terms of Quebec's secession. Preston Manning was in fact ready to treat the barest of majority results as a valid mandate to arrange Quebec's departure from the federation.

"We had talked about accepting the result and not even with a result as high as 52 percent. In the absence of any clear statement from the government as to what it considers a clear question, as to what it considers a clear majority, you have to assume that 50 percent plus 1 would have been enough.

"Chrétien had this communications trick of saying that he would not let the country break up over one vote. But it would not have been just one vote; it would have been four million and thirteen votes versus four million and twelve votes. From a democratic point of view we would have had to stick with that.

"If you were not going to recognize 50 percent plus 1, then say what it is that you will recognize because you can never say that afterwards. By then your moral authority to say anything would have completely evaporated. Our position would have been—perhaps because we were almost as much small-d democrats as we were conservatives or reformers—that you cannot take this position that I accept the results of the referendum if they go my way and I don't accept them when they don't."

Manning would have demanded an election on the morning after a Yes vote, and this was the rationale his Reform Party planned to use to win over Canadians. He expected that there would be a receptive audience for his message. In the weeks and months before the Quebec vote, he had initiated a conversation with Canadians about his party's tough position. Indeed, for a long time the Reform Party and its leader were the only ones who would openly broach the potential consequences of Quebec's secession in the House of Commons. In the period leading up to the referendum, Preston Manning and most of his MPs had taken that sobering show on the road across the country, but not in Quebec.

Only a handful of Reformers—including Stephen Harper—spoke fluent French, but the No forces kept even them at bay. "We could not contribute to the campaign. We were just crippled that way. We had no base there and our reputation was that we were anti-Quebec," says Manning.

In Quebec, the Reform Party was best known for its opposition to the federal Official Languages Act, the regime put in place under Pierre Trudeau in the late sixties. The party argued that official bilingualism was a costly imposition on the regions of the country where French was not commonly used and sought to replace it with a territory-based language policy. Its net effect would have been to limit the use of French by and within the federal government to Quebec and some regions of Atlantic Canada and Ontario.

That Reform policy was a less than stellar calling card on the referendum trail; the notion that Quebec should stay in a federation that had less and less time for the province's majority language was, to say the least, not helping federalist forces make their case to a people that had already seen too many false starts at accommodating their differences.

When the party's social conservatism and its anti-abortion creed were added to the mix, the result was even more unpalatable (Quebec had been the first province to shrug off the Criminal Code restrictions on abortion, a decade before the rest of Canada, and the majority of its people had no wish to turn back the clock.) And so Manning spent the campaign holding meetings in other parts of the country to talk about Canada's future with or without Quebec. What he heard from the public helped shape his conviction that the Liberal days in power would be numbered if Chrétien failed to win the referendum: "Based on the kind of talk I heard in Atlantic Canada and the West, I did not think they would have given a mandate to these people who had just brought the federation to this defeat."

In total, Manning visited seventy communities, answering some ten thousand questions along the way. He figured that had given him a good read on the probable post-Yes mood of the rest of Canada. "The average audience that had not thought about it at all just wanted a Yes or No and let's get on with it whatever the outcome. I did not pick up warm fuzzy feelings toward a negotiation."

The theme of the Reform election campaign that he had in mind for the aftermath of a Yes victory would have been strictly focused on the need for the rest of Canada to organize itself in the wake of Quebec's departure and to figure out the terms of that province's secession.

Manning wasn't interested in trying to persuade Quebecers to back out of a Yes vote. Instead he would have sought to convince voters in the rest of Canada that he was best placed to drive a hard bargain on their behalf. He says he relished the prospect of crossing swords with Bouchard and Parizeau across from a negotiating table. He thought he would have an edge on his Quebec vis-à-vis.

"Western Canada politicians are criticized for not being familiar with Quebec, but I would argue that we had a more realistic assessment of Quebec than Quebec political leaders have of the rest of the country. There is a danger when you are thinking of going into negotiation to not understanding the people who are sitting across from you."

On the Quebec referendum trail, there was little talk of the Reform Party's hardline approach. Federalists did not want to raise the possibility of a Yes victory, and the sovereignist leadership had no interest in casting doubts on its capacity to negotiate a beneficial partnership with Canada.

Those parallel cones of silence frustrated Manning. The rival campaigns in the Quebec referendum agreed on few things, but they seemed to concur in consigning his voice and the input of his party to insignificance. This was true despite—or perhaps because—he had made it his business since his arrival in Parliament to raise alarm bells in both camps. "I'd tell the Bloc: You think when this negotiation occurs that you are going to be sitting across the table from some civilized Toronto lawyer that has bought into bilingualism and biculturalism. But you are going to be sitting across from a steely-eyed lawyer from Calgary who has dealt with sheiks and revolutionaries in South America. You have never been in a negotiation with those types. He is in to defend the interest of provincial governments that are sick and tired of this whole thing. The notion that this will be amicable is a non-starter. It's not going to be like that."

Manning could readily understand why Bouchard and Parizeau would deal with the Reform message with wilful ignorance. To engage him would have been to undermine the case that the Yes camp was making. But he was dumbfounded by the federalist determination to brush him off too.

He and his party had spent the two years since the 1993 election pleading with the Liberal government for a beefed-up federal approach to the referendum debate. "Basically the Reform position was that we should be offering a better form of federalism and a clear understanding of the consequences [of secession]."

Manning started lobbying Jean Chrétien on the Quebec issue during their first private encounter, shortly after that election. "Our basic thrust was that what was needed to deal with the impending secession crisis was a better vision of federalism. There was obviously discontent. We are not going to make it go away by saying the status quo is good enough or by saying we are going to be doing administrative tinkering. We need a better vision of a better federalism.

"I had this discussion with him several times and eventually, I tried to refine it. I would say: Bouchard's got a dream and whether you agree with it or not it's a dream, a vision. You fight dreams and visions with dreams and visions. You do not fight them with administrative stuff. But Chrétien, partly I guess from the context which he came, would insist every time we talked about changing federalism, reforming federalism, that we were talking constitutional change. A lot of the things we were talking about we could accomplish without constitutional change. But he used to equate, at least talking to me, desire to change the way federalism worked with constitutional change.

"The second point I used to make was that the Quebec folks who would vote on this issue needed to be apprised of the consequences, the hard realities of what secession was going to mean. Sovereignists were giving the impression that they would keep every benefit of being part of Canada but that they would be separate. The sooner we disabused them of that the better. Then Chrétien would say that would be provocative and hand sovereignists ammunition."

Manning got nowhere with the prime minister. He says he could not wrestle the beginning of an economic contingency plan from finance minister Paul Martin, and his party also struck out in the House of Commons. "There was no debate in Parliament. We had no discussion that came remotely close to an intellectual debate. We tried to argue that the government should initiate such a debate but Chrétien would respond that this was just providing a forum for separatists. In the House they treated us like we were almost as bad a problem as the Bloc. They said that we were treasonous for raising those questions."

Exacerbated by this ongoing Liberal snub, by October 1995 Manning's unforgiving attitude toward a possible federalist defeat in the referendum was set in stone. He believed that the campaign's near-disastrous turn toward the Yes camp had proven him right.

When all is said and done, his sense that after a Yes vote Canadians would turn against federal politicians from Quebec was closer to the thinking of Chrétien's ROC ministers than to the instinct of the Quebec federalists themselves, who assumed their positions in Parliament would be unaltered and the battle to keep their province in the federation would go on.

Manning's determination to follow up quickly on even a close Yes vote, deal with secession and move on reflected the mood of a significant section of the business community and that of a good many voters, too—including some who had not previously supported the Reform Party. But Manning's approach was not just populist; he had built his hardline position on a solid foundation of self-interest. Before a Yes vote, the Reform Party was crippled by its inability to win votes in Quebec; after a Yes vote, that liability could have been turned into an asset.

After the narrow federalist victory in Quebec, Manning tried to salvage part of his post-Yes narrative. He went hard after Jean Chrétien in the House of Commons for the near-death result of the vote. During the 1997 election, his party ran ads inviting voters to stop supporting parties led by Quebecers.

But Manning overreached. His criticism of Chrétien was blunted by the referendum outcome. Many Canadians felt more relief than residual anger at the country's narrow escape from the turmoil of a Yes vote. The Reform election attack ads on the Charest-led Tories and the Chrétien-led Liberals backfired spectacularly in Ontario, Atlantic Canada and in the national media. On June 2, 1997, the Reform Party again hit a wall at the Manitoba/Ontario border. The rhetoric might have worked wonders for the Reform Party in the climate of a Yes vote, but it rang false after the No camp saved the day. It is a rare family that welcomes the services of a zealous undertaker after a loved one has come out of intensive care and is undergoing a fragile recovery.

In the years immediately following the referendum, most Canadians just wanted to avoid a sequel, fearing an even less happy ending than the 1995 vote. But with that possibility on their minds, many, especially outside Quebec, also craved the more hardline approach to future referendums that Manning had promoted before the 1995 campaign. While the Reform leader shifted his attention from secession rules to a more personal indictment of Chrétien's handling of the referendum and to a renewed push for decentralizing the federation, the Liberals—reading the country's mood—turned the Reform proposals that they used to scoff at into their popular Plan B.

When the Clarity Act was introduced in the House of Commons Manning was not enthused: "I thought: Why now when it is finally over? If this makes sense now would it not have made far more sense to do it in advance of the referendum? And yet proposing it beforehand was denounced as treasonous." It was under pressure from, among others, Stephen Harper—who had by then left politics to head the

National Citizens Coalition—that Manning relented and resolved to support the Liberal act.

In hindsight, Manning sees the referendum period as a "huge once-in-a-lifetime missed opportunity" to rebalance the federation that was lost to Liberal complacency. He is particularly disappointed by the missed chance to reconsider the balance of power between the federal government and the provinces, and what he describes as the political inertia on that front before and after the referendum.

He also believes the referendum episode may have contributed to Stephen Harper leaving politics two years later. "What's the point of staying on when maybe you see something that may be helpful and you can't make it prevail; you just get denounced for putting it forward."

Stephen Harper declined to be interviewed for this book. He is one of the few front-line protagonists from the last referendum who is still active in politics and the only current federal leader who played a leading role in the parliamentary debates surrounding it. Now that he is prime minister, the unity buck stops at his desk. Since 2006 Harper has had the good fortune of not facing the kind of Quebec challenges that defined the tenures of his predecessors. As a result he has mostly kept mum on the issue and on his own role in the 1995 episode.

Stephen Harper was one of the leading architects of the Reform Party's approach to the referendum. He probably spent more time in Quebec during the campaign than any other member of his party and certainly more than his party's unilingual leader. Back then he presumably agreed with Manning's approach to a Yes vote and with the Reform leader's determination to engage in secession talks with Quebec on the basis of a majority Yes vote—no matter how narrow.

A year to the day after the referendum, Harper, in his role as lead Reform critic on the issue, introduced a private member's bill that proposed federal rules for future secession attempts. Bill C–341 called for a clearer question than the convoluted one that was put to Quebecers in 1995, and it stipulated that the threshold for a Yes vote should be 50 percent plus 1.

At the time, Stephen Harper argued that it was Quebec sovereignists and not federal politicians who would feel the fragility of a narrow mandate in negotiations with the rest of Canada. If they insisted on proceeding to secession on a 50-percent-plus-1 basis the long end of the stick in those talks would be in the hands of the ROC, he maintained. It is tough to drive a hard bargain when your mandate to negotiate is so fragile that it might crumble at its first major roadblock.

In early 2013 the question resurfaced in the Commons at the initiative of the NDP and the Bloc Québécois. The New Democrats put forward a bill that paralleled Harper's 1996 initiative. The prime minister and his government declined to engage on the substance of the issue, accusing the opposition parties of dragging Canada back needlessly into the quicksand of referendum politics. But in the fall of the same year, federal lawyers asked the Quebec Superior Court to declare invalid Quebec's Bill 99—a law that spells out the province's right to leave the federation on the basis of a simple majority vote in a referendum.

In 2006, Prime Minister Harper underwent a spectacular conversion on another Quebec-related front when he tabled a resolution in the House of Commons that stipulated that "the Québécois form a nation within a united Canada." Opposition to the recognition of Quebec's distinct status was a cornerstone of the Reform Party, of which he was a founding member. On Harper's watch, the official languages policy that Manning and his early followers had sworn to change has also endured.

In light of the above, it is possible that Harper—now well established in power—has also parted ways with Manning on the minimal threshold for accepting a Yes victory; or at least now that he is prime minister he has found merit in keeping his options open.

PART 4

THE PREMIERS

CHAPTER 13

THINKING OUT OF THE BOX: ROY ROMANOW

U nbeknownst to Jean Chrétien, at least one premier was contemplating radical steps should Quebec opt out of Confederation.

After the return to power of the Parti Québécois in the fall of 1994, Saskatchewan NDP premier Roy Romanow quietly tasked a small group of trusted senior officials to look into the prairie province's options after a sovereignist victory. Filed under the boring title of Constitutional Contingencies—a choice intended to discourage curiosity— its work was funded off the books, outside the provincial Treasury Board process, the better to ensure its secrecy. According to one official who was speaking on background, the fear was that if the existence of the group or its mission were leaked, the story might hurt the federalist cause in Quebec. For the same reason, the full Saskatchewan cabinet was never brought into the loop.

Romanow says he instructed his secret task force to rule out no scenario, including that of Saskatchewan following Quebec out of Canada. "In the eventuality of a Yes vote, clearly you need to examine all your options. Would it be a favoured approach? I guess at some point or other one is forced to make a choice. But we prepared for it. The documentation is around. We did not make a firm decision. I think we were hoping against hope that the thing would work out the way it worked out, for good or for bad."

The committee presented Romanow with a range of options. In all of them, following a Yes vote Saskatchewan would strive to be the master of its own fate. The province would not wait passively for a federal government dominated by Ontario to decide its place and future in a federation without Quebec, nor to define the parameters of a reconfigured Canada without the prairie province's input. Romanow would be prepared to stake out a distinct Saskatchewan position—and to reach out to the other Western Canada provinces, with actual choices in hand, not just pie-in-the-sky rhetoric. "The reality is that you would really have a dysfunctional country in the event of a Yes vote in Quebec. There was no guarantee that what was left over—the rest of Canada—would amount to a functioning entity. How do we deal with Ontario? And what do we do about Atlantic Canada?"

The group examined the merits of adopting the American dollar to protect Saskatchewan from the fallout of a sinking Canadian loonie. Respecting the premier's order to include every option, it did not rule out deeper political ties between the province and the United States. "Would Saskatchewan end up in some alignment with Western Canada and perhaps even drift into a geographic connection with the United States? I would not have wanted a U.S. integration model. It was certainly a foreign thought to me and one I did not accept, but if you look at where the economic ties are placed, even then there was much more of a north–south relationship."

Given a choice and some willing dance partners, Romanow would have preferred that Saskatchewan and the three other Western Canada provinces regroup into a new national entity. From his perspective it was a lesser evil for his small province than getting sucked into the U.S. vortex.

But when Romanow initially broached the idea of contingency plans for the region with Ralph Klein, the Alberta premier ended the discussion before it had even begun. He told his Saskatchewan colleague that thoughts along those lines bordered on treason. "I just could not connect there, although the access was easy. They [Alberta] would answer and they would phone, but there was just a seeming lack of determination to articulate even behind closed doors some possible positions which might even mitigate against a Yes vote. I think there was a misguided belief that it was not going to happen—until toward the very end when polling started to show us that it was very real."

Romanow says his relationships with British Columbia's Glen Clark and Manitoba's Gary Filmon were better than with Klein; but, after the Alberta rebuff, he did not aggressively pursue the issue of a Western union or other hypothetical arrangements with them. However, the Saskatchewan premier did not shut down his committee. The options it had produced were on his mind as he made his way to Montreal to participate in CTV's referendum-night political panel.

If Quebecers voted yes, Romanow's officials believed that the first six to twelve hours would say much about the federal capacity to keep some control of the situation. They would also provide the Saskatchewan government with a sense of whether Jean Chrétien would be able to hang on in the face of a federalist defeat and, if so, for how long.

Like every prime minister who spends time at the first-ministers' table, Jean Chrétien ruffled some feathers and made friends. Among the members of the provincial class of 1995, Roy Romanow was considered his closest ally—on a par with only New Brunswick's Frank McKenna.

Romanow and Chrétien had crossed paths in the constitutional trenches in the early eighties. As ministers of justice in Regina and Ottawa, they were the lead ministers on the patriation file. The friendship endured over the years that followed.

Given those ties, one might assume that Romanow would have been the last premier to start thinking outside the federation box. There is little doubt that the prime minister would not have been overjoyed by his old friend's initiative. Romanow says he did not discuss his search for Saskatchewan's Plan B with Chrétien. Had the Ottawa mandarins who were coordinating the federal referendum strategy been aware of what the Saskatchewan group was working on, they would have urged them to cease and desist immediately. But Romanow persisted, in part because he was also the ROC premier who knew the Parti Québécois best.

Other premiers, such as Gary Filmon, Frank McKenna and Clyde Wells, had been players in the stormy Meech Lake episode. Romanow had sat that one out; his NDP had returned to power in Saskatchewan only in 1991 and by then Brian Mulroney's first constitutional accord had been a year in the grave. But the premiers involved in the Meech Lake debate had dealt with Robert Bourassa, a federalist Quebec premier. Romanow's constitutional baptism by fire in the early eighties had brought him in direct contact with Premier René Lévesque and his cabinet team. That encounter with the PQ and its founding leader was close and sustained over a number of months. Almost until its bitter end, Lévesque and Saskatchewan premier Allan Blakeney (along with every premier except Ontario's Bill Davis and New Brunswick's Richard Hatfield) had played on the same team, throwing provincial roadblocks in the way of Prime Minister Pierre Trudeau to prevent him from patriating the Constitution on his own terms.

Based on that much tougher experience, Romanow took the Parti Québécois and its referendum bid seriously. He did not underestimate what the federalist camp was up against. And in late August 1995 when Jacques Parizeau showed up at his first and only premiers' annual summer retreat in Newfoundland, the Saskatchewan premier's worst fears about Parizeau, but also about most of his provincial colleagues, were confirmed.

"When Parizeau showed up in St. John's, my recollection is that his argument was to try to sell the premiers on this kind of a line that if there were a successful vote for separation or unilateral declaration of independence, intergovernmental relationships would still be maintained. The notion was that common purpose would dictate common sense policies for the survival of the union.

"My line was that this was a total misread of reality and that it was mostly a line to convince Quebecers more so than to convince us that there could be some interprovincial trade and that there would be very limited loss, and that he ought to tell Quebecers that this would not be the case. I can't say I was the only one to respond, but I was certainly the loudest and one of the most obnoxious."

It rattled Romanow to think that Parizeau was using the meeting with his fellow premiers as a backdrop to send a reassuring message about sovereignty to Quebecers, but so did the fact that his provincial counterparts were reluctant to take on their Quebec colleague in public. Newfoundland premier Clyde Wells had played a leading role in the demise of the Meech Lake Accord. He was a highly controversial figure in Quebec. As the host of the meeting, he would normally have been mandated to speak publicly for the group. "For a number of reasons, there was uncertainty about whether a response could only inflame the situation in Quebec."

In the end Romanow addressed the media himself— alone—during a pause in the discussions. He recalls that his break with protocol had precious little impact in Quebec, especially since his rebuttal of Parizeau was delivered only in English. His failure to prompt most of the other premiers into private or public action in anticipation of a possible referendum disaster convinced him that it was best that he keep his own counsel and prepare for the worst.

Romanow knew that if it came to a Yes vote Saskatchewan's back would be more easily broken than those of its more resilient sister provinces. Saskatchewan might not have been as interconnected with Quebec as Ontario was. It would not be separated from what was left of the federation by a different country as Atlantic Canada would be. But it was more vulnerable than average to a post-referendum hit on the Canadian dollar and the country's economy.

"Leaving aside the sentimentality and the emotional dimension [of a Yes vote], we were facing an extremely precarious position in Saskatchewan. The province that I had inherited in 1991 was essentially flat broke. I don't think I'm overstating it. We worried because we were already very fragile. I used to have to go down to New York in those days to show my books to the bankers, and the prospect of a Yes vote would have sunk us with interest rates and the devaluation of the dollar."

In 1995, Saskatchewan had not yet been made affluent by its energy resources. Today it is second only to Alberta for its oil production. But when Roy Romanow had led the NDP back to power in Regina, his province was an economic basket case. Its finances were still so deteriorated that the federal government was threatening to step in to clean up the books. Among the provinces, only Newfoundland was in as dismal a fiscal shape.

"Before Brian Mulroney left office [in 1993] he phoned me about the gravity of the Saskatchewan and Newfoundland situations. The essence of the conversation was that we had to take dramatic action and if we did not, the federal government would have to act and the Bank of Canada governor would have to intervene."

By 1995, Romanow had put the province on a harsh fiscal diet that had included the closure of fifty-two rural hospitals. Things were starting to look up on the budget front, but Saskatchewan was hardly safe from the predictable collateral damage of a Yes vote. "My very big priority was Saskatchewan and how we were going to handle what I knew would be the very negative reactions of the American markets and world markets to this situation."

In the aftermath of a referendum loss, Premier Romanow would suffer no illusion that his rapport with Jean Chrétien would help Saskatchewan. If anything, Chrétien would need Romanow more than the premier would need the prime minister; even proposing that the prime minister remain in office would be a hard sell in Saskatchewan. "In our own planning, Chrétien's legitimacy was a very big consideration. I say this very reluctantly because this is a man [for whom] I have great admiration and I did not tell him at the time, but we in Saskatchewan had been thinking for a couple of weeks that the issue of whether or not he would continue was suddenly problematic.

"How do you explain to the people of Preeceville, Saskatchewan, that a Quebecer is negotiating on our behalf against a Quebecer who is determined to break up the country as we saw it? There is no doubt that it was a big factor."

If he had lost the referendum, Chrétien could have counted on Roy Romanow's public support, but not indefinitely. "That night, there was no other option; we had to buttress the prime minister of the day, at least to my mind. There really was not a very best scenario in such a situation, but that seemed to be the better of a bad lot. I don't know how else in the immediate six months or so we could figure out the economic arrangements without a great deal of economic upset, especially in the absence of a government nationally that could pretend to be national in the circumstances. I did not see how his immediate departure could happen.

"How long he would be able to continue would have been another issue. By the way, I think he must have been contemplating that as well. There was no choice but to put the best face and the best argument forward for Canada on the outcome. But there was the attached concern over what would happen over the next few days or weeks.

"I thought that that night he [Chrétien] must display firm, steady leadership, not indicate by either visible sign or by word that somehow this was a rejection of his national leadership, of not being able to relate to Quebec. It was absolutely important that he continue in a position of leadership, that the argument that he would advance about the result of the vote would be an argument that would point to the result being inconclusive."

After the referendum, Romanow urged Chrétien to resist calls for his resignation. In spite of the very close federalist victory, the Saskatchewan premier held faith with his friend. "Even though his leadership may have been damaged for a while, he had to continue to exhibit the determination and the vision to see his way through this narrow result. I think it is the kind of guy he is."

Romanow says the two of them did not discuss the referendum after it was over. He did not, after the fact, revisit his very real grievances about the referendum process with Chrétien. "To this day, I have never sat down with the prime minister and reflected on the experience. I think he feels that the end result speaks for itself."

If Romanow had wanted to lick old referendum wounds with anyone he would have found Preston Manning—a fellow westerner—to be a more sympathetic audience than his old friend in Ottawa. The former prairie premier and the founder of the Reform Party spent the campaign preaching the same gospel in a common desert.

On paper, Roy Romanow and Preston Manning are political worlds apart. The first is a New Democrat from the prairie province that started Canada's love affair with national social programs by inventing medicare. The second is a proudly right-wing Albertan whose father, Ernest Manning, was once the Social Credit premier of Canada's most conservative province.

But when it comes to the 1995 referendum their experiences are eerily similar. Neither speaks French fluently, a feature that has always severely limited their capacity to engage Quebecers. And both dragged behind them too much constitutional baggage to be of much use to the federalist forces in Quebec anyway. The Reform Party was in disrepute in Quebec for having opposed Brian Mulroney's constitutional efforts and, more specifically, the recognition of the province's distinct character. Romanow, of course, was unpopular for supporting Pierre Trudeau at the time of patriation.

In Quebec, Romanow's role in the final negotiation of the 1982 patriation deal has been maligned for as long it has been praised in other Canadian quarters. The enduring Quebec narrative holds that the patriation of the Constitution resulted from a collective act of betrayal perpetrated against René Lévesque. The seven premiers who had pledged to negotiate shoulder-to-shoulder with Quebec at the constitutional table—including Saskatchewan's Allan Blakeney—are said to have conspired at the last minute, stabbing Lévesque in the back in the dead of an Ottawa night. In Quebec, where memories die hard, suspicions borne of *la nuit des longs couteaux*, or "the night of the long knives," as it is known, endured.

Romanow was reminded of that when he caught a live broadcast of the last big rally of the Yes campaign. From his

Saskatchewan home, he watched Lucien Bouchard mimic Jean Chrétien on the phone, taking his marching orders from various premiers. The first caller was Clyde Wells—the premier who had most staunchly opposed the Meech Lake Accord. The next one—Bouchard announced—was Roy Romanow. It is a scene the former Saskatchewan premier will never forget. "As soon as my name was mentioned there was on television this absolute avalanche of boos that seemed to be running on forever. I thought I was going to have a heart attack. I yelled to my wife, 'Quick, come, you have to see this.' I did not fall off the couch but it sure punctured me. I felt absolutely devastated by it all."

So devastated, in fact, that Romanow declined to travel to Montreal to take part in the October 27 pro-Canada rally. "I was invited, not very warmly but sufficiently. I was very conscious of the fact that my presence could exacerbate what we knew by then was a very close contest. So I did not go.

"In some ways I felt handicapped and neutered and frustrated, not because of the effective campaign speeches that Bouchard and others were delivering but by the impression of the night of the long knives. To get into this kind of a debate and defend myself in 1995 when the vote was so close would only have inflamed everybody who was involved. It is a little frustration that I still carry."

But it was not Romanow's only frustration. Like Manning, the Saskatchewan premier had pleaded with Jean Chrétien (and with the other premiers) for a different—more aggressive—federal approach to the referendum campaign. "I would have hoped that we would say two things to

Quebec: we can work something out to achieve some of your objectives—maybe not those of Mr. Parizeau and Bouchard—but you also must know that this course that you are on is fraught with great risks.

"We should have communicated to Quebec the consequences . . . For everybody in this kind of a bust-up nothing is easy. Whether it's custody, sharing of assets and the institutions, nothing is easy. I would have thought that it would be a useful position to put out there but it was not. I don't know why it was not. On the basis of the analysis that I had done, it bothered me very much."

For all of their ideological differences, Romanow and Manning were in agreement with each other and at odds with Chrétien on referendum strategy. In the aftermath of a federalist defeat, they might well have stayed that way.

After a Yes vote, Romanow was willing to give Chrétien more wiggle room than Manning was. But that could have forced the premier to swim against the tide of public opinion in his own province. In 1995, Saskatchewan had little presence in the Liberal government of Jean Chrétien. The Reform Party held most of the province's seats. After a federalist defeat, Manning's argument that Chrétien and his team could not be trusted to speak for the West or for the rest of Canada, for that matter, would have resonated there.

When it came to defending the interests of his province at the secession-negotiation table, Romanow moved closer to the Reform leader's hardline position. He might have been less blunt about it than Manning, but he was not about to let Chrétien's federal government speak for Saskatchewan. "We very strongly felt that the provinces would have to be involved in those next steps. This was not a Quebec/Ottawa situation, this was a Quebec/Ottawa/Regina/you-name-it situation. It's the federation that was involved. I'm not sure where Ottawa stood on this thing, whether they would have wanted to have additional voices of the federation around, but that was our position."

After the referendum, Roy Romanow became a vocal supporter of the federal Clarity Act. He put pressure on the federal NDP and its leader, Alexa McDonough, to support it. She had initially been reluctant to come out in favour of Jean Chrétien's main post-referendum initiative. When she did side with the Clarity Act authors, her decision caused consternation in some NDP quarters.

Her successor, Jack Layton, distanced the party from the Liberal law. In early 2013, the federal New Democrats under Thomas Mulcair, the party's first leader from Quebec, presented a bill to repeal the Clarity Act. Mulcair was not Romanow's choice to replace Layton. On the Clarity Act, Romanow and Mulcair do not see eye to eye, and their differences account in no small part for the fact that the two sometimes seem as distant from each other as if they did not belong to the same party.

In the years after the referendum, Romanow also worked to make sure that if ever there was a pro-secession vote in Quebec, the provinces would have a say in the process of redrawing the federation. When the federal government referred the issue of Quebec secession to the Supreme Court for judicial guidance in 1997, Saskatchewan was one of just two provinces—with Manitoba—to present arguments to the top court. Those arguments dealt with the constitutional right of the provinces to be party to any secession negotiation. Romanow's referendum concerns—that provinces like his would be ignored in the turmoil that would follow a Yes vote—found their way into the comprehensive 1998 Supreme Court opinion that formed part of the basis for the Clarity Act. That ruling affirmed Quebec's constitutional right to secede from the federation but stipulated that it had to do so within a mutually agreed referendum framework that included a clear question and a clear majority result. If those conditions were met, the Court concluded that the federal government and the provinces would have a duty to at least engage in negotiations with Quebec.

CHAPTER 14

A NEW ONTARIO PARADIGM: MIKE HARRIS

As he sat in his Queen's Park office awaiting the results of the Quebec referendum, Ontario premier Mike Harris was aware of four sobering realities.

The first was that if the sovereignist vote won in Quebec, it was going to be sink or swim time for his rookie provincial government. Little during the few months that he and his team had been in power had prepared them to plunge headlong into the worst unity crisis in modern Canadian history.

The second was that even if, as Harris tended to believe, a sovereignist victory did not lead to Quebec's independence, Ontario, like all of Canada, was in for a year or more of chaos. There was little that the premier of the country's most populous province could do about that.

The third and possibly most galling consideration was that the fate of his Common Sense Revolution—the right-wing platform his Progressive Conservatives had run on that spring—was suddenly in the hands of Quebec voters. If Quebecers gave the Parti Québécois a pro-sovereignty mandate, Harris's plans to rewrite the social contract between Queen's Park and Ontario voters—his ambition to reverse half a century of governmental expansionism by downsizing the provincial government—would be lost in the shuffle of a national crisis.

Finally, the premier feared that Prime Minister Jean Chrétien and his government did not have the beginning of a game plan to deal with the mess of a Yes vote. If they did, Harris was not aware of it. And at a time when he was still breaking in his new shoes at Queen's Park, Harris was himself ill equipped to fill a possible federal leadership vacuum.

Mike Harris had only been in office for 120 days. His cabinet and caucus were still on training wheels. Nationally, he was the new kid on the block. Prior to its June victory, the Progressive Conservative Party had been out of power at Queen's Park for a decade. During his fourteen years in the provincial arena, the MPP from Nipissing who now led the party had spent only four actually governing—at the very beginning of his tenure in the Ontario legislature.

Harris had first been elected a year after the 1980 Quebec referendum and had followed the fifteen-year constitutional war that had led to this second vote on Quebec's future largely from the opposition sidelines. Few of his ministers had been in office the last time a Tory premier from Ontario had played a role in a major constitutional episode. In the early eighties, Bill Davis had been Pierre Trudeau's staunchest ally in his effort to patriate the Constitution, but Harris had been too junior an MPP to have had a part in that play.

If the Yes side won in Quebec now, Ontario's untested premier would be going into a mega-unity crisis without a script. The advisers who had helped him cross from opposition to the premier's office were as short of the necessary expertise as he was. None of them was a constitutional wonk and most were actually proud of it. They had little or no time for the discussion that has monopolized Canada's political class for the best part of their adult lives. Win or lose, Plan A for Harris on referendum night was to avoid getting sucked into what he describes as "the distraction of the constitutional vortex."

But that did not mean that the premier planned to go blind into the post-referendum fog. In the lead-up to the campaign he had secured the services of two battle-hardened constitutional warriors. While Harris and his lieutenants watched the results on CTV, Richard Dicerni and Hugh Segal sat in a different corner of his office suites to follow the proceedings on Radio-Canada.

As a francophone, Dicerni had naturally tuned in to the French network. Segal had joined him because, as a bilingual former Montrealer, he knew that any English-language station would obscure Quebec's actual post-referendum pulse with Canadian anguish.

Many years before taking a deputy minister's post at Queen's Park, Richard Dicerni had spent the 1980 referendum in the federal backrooms, toiling away on the Quebec campaign as executive director of the Information Centre on Canadian Unity—the unit tasked with crafting and massaging Pierre Trudeau's federal referendum message. Later, he had found his way into the federal civil service; when Lucien Bouchard had been sworn in as secretary of state in Brian Mulroney's cabinet in 1988, Dicerni had worked with the Progressive Conservative government's new Quebec star. Then, prior to coming to work for Ontario's NDP government in 1992, Dicerni had been deputy secretary of the federal-provincial relations desk—a front-row seat on the pre-referendum scene. Dicerni had left Ottawa before Jean Chrétien took power, but he knew all the main players inside and outside the unity bureaucracy and he understood its culture.

"He was absolutely the right person at that time," says Harris. "I was a newly elected premier. My political team had very little knowledge of Quebec. We had just come in. We were in a fiscal crisis. We were embarking on a major fiscal correction. That is where our head was."

Hugh Segal had been a senior aide to Premier Davis at the time of patriation. He had served Brian Mulroney as chief of staff over the period of the final negotiation of the 1992 Charlottetown Accord and the federal referendum that followed. A lifelong Tory with a politically ecumenical bent, Segal did not lack for Liberal contacts in high places; a decade after the referendum, Prime Minister Paul Martin would appoint him to the Senate.

On referendum night, Harris had yet to have a single meeting of substance with Chrétien. He had attended his first summer gathering of the premiers in August and his arrival on the scene had largely been eclipsed by Jacques Parizeau's sovereignty talk.

Over the course of the referendum campaign, most of the federal intelligence that filtered down to Queen's Park and its newly installed premier was funnelled in by Segal and Dicerni. The information they gathered did not add up to a pretty picture for the federalist cause.

In the lead-up to the 1980 referendum, Pierre Trudeau had taken little for granted. On his government's orders, federal bureaucrats had sketched out contingency plans to deal with a federalist defeat. Not in 1995. Complacency was a factor. The No camp was long convinced a win was in the bag and the polling numbers had backed up its confident forecast. But another element was also at play.

In 1980, Jean Chrétien—then Trudeau's lead minister on the referendum trail in Quebec—had resented the energy that the civil service had expended on worst-case scenarios, fearing their work would backfire in Quebec by suggesting a lack of confidence within the federalist camp. So anxious had the planning made him, he'd wanted briefing notes on the matter shredded to prevent any chance of a leak. Chrétien was not so politically naive as to take a victory for granted. But if worse came to worst, he reasoned, there would be time enough to regroup after the vote. On his prime ministerial watch fifteen years later, his approach toward weighing federal options in the event of a Yes vote prevailed.

From the perspective of Queen's Park, Chrétien's strategy was a worrisome development. His political position in the event of a Yes vote would have been significantly more fragile than Trudeau's in 1980 and he stood to have a lot less room to manoeuvre in Quebec. Trudeau had just won a majority mandate in an election that had seen his Liberals paint Quebec red. They came out of that campaign with seventy-four of the province's seventy-five seats and every single Quebec MP was a federalist. If he had lost that first referendum, Trudeau would not have lacked for Liberal boots on the Quebec ground to execute a federalist counteroffensive.

In 1995 Chrétien did not enjoy the same advantage. His power base was in Ontario, where his party had most recently won every seat but one. In the 1993 election only a handful of Quebec francophone ridings had elected Liberal MPs. The Bloc Québécois owned most of the province's francophone territory and in the House of Commons Lucien Bouchard—not the prime minister—could claim to speak for the most Quebec voters.

With referendum day looming, Harris had Richard Dicerni keep very close track of the evolving federal strategy. He found it increasingly erratic. By referendum night, the premier's informed impression was that the late federalist scramble in Quebec had sucked up all the oxygen at the expense of contingency planning.

In the last weeks of the campaign, official Ottawa was in a state of institutionalized panic. As Harris and his advisers tried to think their way through the potential fallout for Ontario of a sovereignist referendum victory, it seemed to them that the federal thinking did not extend beyond the immediate night of the vote itself: "We sensed there would be no national response," recalls the premier. He could get no solid take on Chrétien's plans and suspected that the other premiers were as much in the dark about the federal intentions as he was. "I think that in the eyes of the prime minister we were probably irrelevant until after the vote."

Harris said he got a full measure of just how right he was when Chrétien travelled to Verdun to deliver that last pre-referendum speech in the final week of the campaign. Desperate for a game-changer, the prime minister belatedly promised to devolve more powers to the provinces, which was long hoped for by Harris and fellow premiers such as Alberta's Ralph Klein. But the core of Chrétien's speech dealt with that more Quebec-centric issue of the constitutional recognition of the province's distinct character.

The federal government had not secured Ontario's agreement—formal or otherwise—to reopen the distinct society debate or the Constitution, nor had it even sought the provincial government's advice on either. If it had, the federal Liberals would have been warned off in the strongest terms. Premier Harris was adamant that he would not re-enter the constitutional fray. His two predecessors, David Peterson and Bob Rae, had each spent a lot of political capital in vain on the issue of distinct society and he had no interest in doing the same.

Almost a decade after it had first appeared in the 1987 Meech Lake Accord, the distinct society idea had lost its shine in the eye of the Ontario public. It had initially been seen as a gesture of goodwill to Quebec, but by 1995 the notion was polarizing the Ontario electorate. Harris was convinced that, for a substantial number of his constituents, any move on that front would be dead on arrival.

"We liked the message from the Verdun speech of power-sharing. That was part of my mantra. We did not like the side where Chrétien was talking about distinct society and alluding to some kind of constitutional round. We were not going to sit down and negotiate anything constitutional. The feds might, but they were not doing it with Ontario."

During the campaign, Harris had used the business luncheon venue of Toronto's Canadian Club to stake out Ontario's position vis-à-vis a possible Yes vote. The opposition leaders had vetted his speech beforehand. Former NDP premier Bob Rae—Harris's immediate predecessor—had given input on its content. Before delivering the speech, Harris had gone through the text paragraph by paragraph with Dicerni, paying extra attention to which sections he would read in French and which in English.

The premier might have been new to the Quebec/Canada debate but he had no interest in his province becoming a mere bystander in the referendum conversation. "We wanted it to be clear that this was a unified message from all of Ontario, a non-partisan message."

The speech cast a Yes vote as a vote for Quebec's separation from Canada. It rejected out of hand a future Quebec/Canada political and economic partnership along the lines proposed in the referendum question. "There was no in-between. We did not want Quebecers to buy into the notion of giving the equivalent of a strong strike mandate, a strong negotiating position. Bouchard was good at selling that. It had strong resonance. We did not want that. If it was a Yes vote, we were not in the mood to be generous in negotiating any term that allowed some kind of union. The message was: don't think those negotiations are going to lead to a happy situation."

Anyone listening to that speech could have concluded that Ontario, in the face of a Yes referendum victory, would agree to Quebec's departure from the federation—much like Ontario's, and Quebec's, corporate movers and shakers—albeit on the terms that served the province best. Indeed, when Harris had some of his people informally sound out corporate and civil society opinion leaders in the dying days of the campaign, his feelers failed to turn up any appetite for prolonging the uncertainty that would result from a pro-sovereignty outcome, even in the name of "saving the country."

In spite of his public stance, Harris says that if the sovereignist camp had won, Ontario would not actually have rushed to the conclusion that Quebec was headed for the exit. "We probably would then have switched the interpretation of the vote to say that was a pretty unclear question. Here is our position: Canada is not going anywhere." In retrospect, it seems that there was a fair dose of posturing involved in the Ontario doctrine that the premier had articulated at the Canadian Club. There was an "in-between" to be explored after all.

Harris says he did not entirely rule out the possibility that Quebec and Canada would enter into secession talks. But he believed that if it came to that, the most likely result would be to turn Quebecers off sovereignty. "Parizeau meant business, but if he was to follow the referendum with a year or a year and a half of failed negotiations, he would not succeed. We did not think that anything he got was going to be acceptable. That's why we believed we were in for a year of chaos. At some point we would have said to Quebecers: over the past year you have learned that you are not going to have the dollar; you are not going to have this or that. I don't believe that Quebecers, knowing all this would have continued to support sovereignty."

Harris admits that there were potential cracks in the Ontario armour. For one, the premier feared that "the chaos could be used against us, against the rest of Canada and reinforce Quebecers' determination to leave." He also doubted that the federal government had the fortitude to lead the country through the morass of a post-Yes vote.

"I was concerned about the concentration of power in Quebec ministers. We were afraid that Chrétien, because he was a Quebecer, was going to be an appeaser. We were afraid he would emphasize distinct society and embark us on a constitutional round that we did not believe in."

But Harris adds that he never gave regime change in Ottawa much thought. He had to have known that Preston Manning was eager to step up and take over from the Chrétien Liberals. But Manning held no seats in Ontario, and it was far from certain that the province's voters would readily embrace the leader of a party dominated by Western Canada to lead so sensitive a negotiation on their behalf.

"There was discussion on that but we had no control over it. What would happen in Ottawa was not heavy on our minds. What was heavy on our minds was Ontario's position and response. Referendum aside, we felt we were facing an uncertain future, and getting our economy back on track was uppermost in our minds. There would be no unifying voice. I don't believe it would have been possible to get agreement among the premiers across the country as to who would have been speaking for Canada."

Looking to a year of post-referendum chaos, the premier was more concerned about his capacity to lead a united Ontario through that period than he was about possible divisions at the federal level. "Our own people might just say the hell with it. There would be some who would say give them whatever they want. And there would be others who would say no, let them go."

The referendum episode was as brief as it was intense for Harris. It barely spanned the first few months of his two-mandate reign. In the wake of the federalist victory in Quebec, the premier and his team promptly turned their minds back to implementing the platform on which they had been elected.

But on Parliament Hill and at Queen's Park, the ripples of the referendum episode—despite its federalist ending— did not abate, changing the relationship between the federal government and its Ontario partner for years to come.

———

When it comes to constitutional reform, Ontario's political class has a long, consensual history. At Queen's Park, in contrast with the legislatures of New Brunswick, Manitoba, Newfoundland or, for that matter, the Quebec National Assembly, the Meech Lake Accord did not become a defining, wedge issue. New Democrats, Liberals and Tories have usually strived to keep constitutional matters out of the partisan arena.

At the time of the patriation of the Constitution, the opposition parties generally supported Premier Davis's efforts and they celebrated the outcome of the talks. When the New Democrats replaced the Liberals in power shortly after the demise of the Meech Lake Accord, Bob Rae led Ontario back to the constitutional table and picked up where his predecessor, David Peterson, had left off. In 1992 the two other main Ontario parties joined Rae's NDP in supporting the Charlottetown Accord, albeit with varying degrees of enthusiasm.

Over the successful and less successful constitutional rounds of the previous decades, the constitutional current between Ottawa and Queen's Park had flowed continuously, regardless of tensions between the two governments on several other fronts. David Peterson and Brian Mulroney clashed over the 1988 free trade agreement with the United States but over the same period they worked hand in hand on Meech Lake. Bob Rae and the federal Tories had conflicting outlooks on the economy but they still cooperated at the constitutional table.

After the 1995 referendum the longstanding Ottawa/ Queen's Park constitutional connection was broken.

The dust had barely settled on the Quebec vote when Jean Chrétien and Mike Harris finally sat for a first serious face-to-face conversation. It did not go well. The prime minister wanted to follow up on his Verdun promise to Quebecers to move on the constitutional recognition of the province as a distinct society. He needed Ontario's support to do so. Premier Harris was determined not to give it.

"It was astounding to me and to our people that he [Chrétien] had no idea where we would stand on that. We were completely shocked that he thought it was a good idea. We thought it was the stupidest thing we had ever heard. We thought: we just avoided this chaos and he is going to throw us back in it.

"We were stunned about the ask and they were stunned about the reaction. It was a pretty blunt no. I guess I expected more of the prime minister of the day. We did not have a good relationship after that for quite a while. The meeting contributed to a lot of bitterness."

In retrospect Chrétien should have known better.

Premiers Davis, Peterson and Rae had spent entire mandates consumed by the constitutional file, with ever diminishing political returns. Harris did not want to go down the same path, not with the odds of a positive outcome so low. Until the dying days of the referendum campaign, Chrétien himself had argued that the Constitution should be left alone;

the Ontario premier was echoing the prime minister's mantra, one he had abandoned only in the campaign's late hours, and only then because he was scrambling to avoid a defeat.

Harris's advisers believed that reopening the issue of distinct society was the equivalent of throwing a match in a tinderbox. They were not thinking just of volatile Quebec. The risks that a resumption of the debate over Quebec's distinctive character would ignite passions in Ontario were real. The entire bid could easily backfire on the federalist camp and possibly create the winning conditions Lucien Bouchard needed to head right back to the referendum trail—and win.

The end of the previous constitutional round had shown Ontario's political leadership to be increasingly out of step with a growing segment of the province's public opinion. In spite of the commendations of their political, media and business establishments, only a slight majority of Ontarians endorsed the Charlottetown Accord in the 1992 federal plebiscite.

Even before that vote it had been apparent that the distinct society issue had become a lightning rod around which anti-Quebec sentiments coalesced. They may have been the work of a minority of zealots, but toward the end of the Meech Lake episode some of the events that had most exacerbated nationalist passions in Quebec had unfolded in neighbouring Ontario.

There had been the Brockville stomping of a Quebec flag. In more normal circumstances the incident would have been dismissed as the action of a few crackpots, but in the feverish atmosphere of the spring of 1990 it became Exhibit A of English Canada's intolerance toward Quebec's language and culture.

There also was the adoption by a number of Ontario municipalities of English-only resolutions designed to absolve them from the obligation to provide services in French. That obligation was essentially a figment of the imagination of the Alliance for the Preservation of English Canada (APEC), an anti-bilingualism lobby group. Localities that no one in Quebec could have previously placed on a map were suddenly the stuff of front-page headlines. Some of those municipalities were not even covered by a new Ontario law that expanded French-language provincial (and not municipal) services. The francophone proportion of their population was well below the bill's 10 percent threshold for providing such services. But others—like Sault Ste. Marie— were home to longstanding francophone communities.

In Ontario politics, the Progressive Conservatives had traditionally harboured the largest number of staunch opponents to French-language rights. During the late sixties, the resistance in Ontario to Trudeau's introduction of official bilingualism had been most vocal in Tory-held ridings, some of which saw local bids to establish French-language schools repeatedly degenerate into pitched battles between Franco-Ontarian parents and anglophone school boards.

The Constitution prescribes that French and English shall have equal footing in the Quebec National Assembly and in the province's court system and that the province's laws shall be published in both languages. After the 1980 referendum, Prime Minister Trudeau had tried to persuade Premier Davis, a Progressive Conservative, to accept the same constitutional obligations for Ontario.

Davis had turned him down but it was not because he opposed the substance of those obligations. Davis's attorney-general, Roy McMurtry, was a proactive francophile. On Davis's watch French-language rights had steadily been expanded in Ontario—most notably in the province's school system. But the premier feared that any grand symbolic move of the kind that Trudeau was after would result in a major backlash. And if that happened, his Tory party—given some of its less tolerant voices—would be in the eye of the storm.

Jean Chrétien was Roy McMurtry's federal vis-à-vis at the time of the patriation debate. The two became friends. Given that, Chrétien would have been familiar with the less than easy history of the Ontario Tories with the Quebec issue and the French-language rights debate. In the middle of the 1980 referendum campaign, Davis had even needed to step in to end a festering local controversy over the building of a French-language high school in Penetanguishene, fearing irreparable damage to the federalist cause in Quebec.

By 1995, Harris had yet another reason to keep his government at a safe distance from the constitutional minefield. His Tories worried that the Reform Party might be about to launch a provincial branch in Ontario. The premier says he asked Tony Clement—who had been a top aide in his office prior to becoming an MPP—to liaise with the Reform Party. Clement's mission was to keep the peace between the two parties and, more importantly, to keep Manning's followers from setting their sights on Queen's Park. That temptation would have increased exponentially if Harris had signed on to Chrétien's distinct society initiative.

Preston Manning had always opposed plans to formally recognize Quebec as a distinct society. That opposition had been one of the founding tenets of his party and one of its main attractions to scores of converts. The referendum had not changed his stance on the issue. To at least partly follow up on his referendum commitment to Quebecers, Jean Chrétien eventually brought a parliamentary resolution on distinct society to the House of Commons. The Reform Party fought that resolution tooth and nail. It passed with the support of the Liberals and the NDP.

As an aside, Harris's refusal to jump back into the constitutional fray was largely validated a decade later when Prime Minister Stephen Harper brought in his Quebec nation resolution. The move was described in apocalyptic terms in some media quarters. There were dire predictions that the motion somehow heralded the end of the country as Canadians knew it. The only saving grace of that overheated debate was that it lasted for only the few days that it took the House of Commons to adopt the motion and not the months and years that it might have taken to insert Jean Chrétien's distinct society amendment into the Constitution.

During the referendum campaign, Premier Harris worked hard to ensure that opposition parties at Queen's Park didn't stray from his party's stance on the Quebec debate. Up to a point, he did so out of self-interest. Many Ontarians would have frowned at a premier who came across as an amateur on the unity stage. In the event of a Yes vote, Harris was determined to maintain an all-party consensus on the way forward.

But after the referendum, the longstanding practice that has seen Ontario and Ottawa protect each other's back in the constitutional trenches did not endure. That tacit alliance had provided the momentum for constitutional reform. In its wake the very concept of the first ministers coming together to hash out ambitious federal-provincial designs fell out of fashion. Over his near decade as prime minister Stephen Harper has spent more time at the G8 table than at the federal-provincial one.

CHAPTER 15

EMERGENCY REPAIRS: FRANK MCKENNA

I n the dying days of the referendum campaign, New Brunswick premier Frank McKenna had a startling conversation with Prime Minister Jean Chrétien. "He called me. He was quite anxious. Generally speaking Chrétien is a real optimist, sometimes falsely optimistic, but he was very anxious. He asked if I would be prepared to serve in a national unity cabinet. He told me: Look, if things go badly we are going to have to react to this. Would you be prepared to do this?"

Chrétien mentioned that he was contemplating making a similar approach to other provincial politicians, notably Saskatchewan's Roy Romanow. "He was trying to put together a list of people who would have some legitimacy and would quiet the country down as we tried to figure this thing out. The prime minister was looking for a political response to try to counteract the attacks that would be made on him. If he had lost, there would have been a hostile reaction beyond the imagination of almost all of us in the rest of Canada. The unity cabinet would have been a diversion as people settled down and took a deep breath. It would have been an escape valve."

The New Brunswick premier did not hesitate: "I confess that my answer was yes. It was just one of those situations where your country needs you and you do what you have to do. I was very happy being premier of New Brunswick, but this was something that seemed very important. It struck me that this was a situation where it was late in the game, things were going badly, and this was an idea that was being thrown out there to settle the Canadian public after a bad result. It would have had to happen quickly."

Chrétien's call confirmed McKenna's worst fears. He was the only sitting premier fluent enough in French to have spent time productively on the referendum campaign trail. In Canada, New Brunswick comes second only to Quebec for the bilingual capacity of its politicians. About one-third of New Brunswickers have French as their mother tongue, a proportion higher than in any province outside Quebec. At one point in the referendum campaign, McKenna says, his entire cabinet had hit the road in eastern Quebec, the region that abuts New Brunswick. "Based on what my ministers were hearing and seeing, I'd come to the conclusion that we were likely to lose the referendum."

A Yes vote was an ominous prospect for New Brunswick, one that came with no silver lining. "The Maritimes would be screwed. The rest of Canada had its own economic engines but we did not. Economically we would have looked at it as the equivalent of a wall of Berlin going up between New Brunswick and the rest of Canada. Our closest market would be a hostile one. Quebec was protectionist at the worst of times. It could only get worse after separation."

There was also the matter of New Brunswick's large Acadian community, which is French speaking. "This would have been profoundly threatening to the Acadians. Within New Brunswick it would have reignited linguistic passions that we had put to rest. With the province on the other side of the fault line and because of our dual linguistic communities, we would have been impacted more than any other part of Canada."

McKenna fully expected Jean Chrétien to resist a Yes vote. "I think we would have had a stalemate. We would have said: We have never agreed that this was the proper question, never agreed that this was the appropriate number of people who need to vote. We would have settled in a state of paralysis. I don't know who would have blinked first."

He also thought that if Chrétien was going to have a chance of staying on and repairing the damage of a referendum defeat, the prime minister would have to talk tough to his fellow Quebecers. "As a Quebec prime minister there is no doubt there would have been a lot of suspicion about him in the rest of the country. I think because of that he would have had to be even more hostile to Quebec [than a non-Quebec PM], but I doubt he could have caught up to the level of hostility of public opinion, particularly in Western Canada."

Frank McKenna was prepared to do his bit on referendum night to help buy the federal government enough breathing room that Chrétien could recast his cabinet—and give himself time to figure out how he as premier would juggle his dual federal and New Brunswick responsibilities following the federalist defeat. "The theme of my remarks if the result would have gone against the country was essentially that Quebecers have spoken this evening. It's my view that we need to let some time pass and let the blood stop boiling and leave the porch light on and not overreact. My central theme was: Let's just catch our breath and leave the door open because this thing is far from over."

McKenna felt that casting his lot with the sitting prime minister made more sense than the alternative. He could tie his political ship to one that was listing badly, or he could hand over responsibility for setting terms of secession between Canada and Quebec to Preston Manning's Reform Party. And he wasn't going to let that happen without a fight.

McKenna was a fiscally conservative Liberal, but Manning's brand of social conservatism was alien to his political culture. He was convinced that if it were put to them, a majority of ROC voters would refuse the Reform Party a mandate to usher Quebec out of the federation. "Nobody would ever forgive the government of Canada for negotiating the secession of a province, and especially with a [referendum] result that was ambiguous and vague and narrow. The rest of Canada would have considered that Preston Manning was being treasonous," he argues.

Further, McKenna doubted that Manning's predominantly Western caucus had the capacity to represent the interests of the whole country fairly. "Ontario and Atlantic Canada very much wanted Quebec to stay because we are neighbours, we're relatives, we're friends, we're trading partners. Western Canada would have said: Let them go, end of story. The farther you go west, the more vicious the view would be."

McKenna knew that Chrétien would face an uphill battle to survive a Yes vote in Quebec, but assembling a national unity cabinet offered him at least a fighting chance. "If he had the right people, people with credibility, I think that it would have worked better than the status quo. The prime minister having lost the referendum would have had a lot of credibility trouble in the nation and I thought it was a sensible idea. Whether it would work or not, I don't know, but I thought it was a sensible alternative."

During the lead-up to the referendum campaign, McKenna—unlike Roy Romanow—had not asked officials to develop contingency plans for his province. But contingencies were nonetheless on his mind. "I would have started thinking selfishly very quickly because we would have been a very vulnerable region. A Maritime union would have been likely. We would have had to get our finances in shape very quickly, rig our ship for tough sailing. We would have had to have free trade within our region. We would have had to make ourselves strong and self-sufficient and would have had to strengthen our trade ties with the United States and, in fact, grow a lot closer to the New England states. We would go much further down that road."

McKenna did not believe that Atlantic Canada could or should try to band together and go it alone after a Yes vote, but he was not predisposed to look to Lucien Bouchard's offer of a political and economic partnership for New Brunswick's salvation. Instead, in the worst-case scenario of Quebec's actual departure, the premier fully intended to find new building blocks for his region's economy in the debris of the break-up. "I would go after vulnerable industries in Quebec. I would go after those like the aerospace industry that rely on government of Canada procurement practices. I would try to move those out of Quebec and into my province. If the government of Canada was going to keep their procurement policies for Canadian companies, there is no reason why many of them would need to continue to be in Quebec.

"I would seek to have some Quebec military bases relocated to New Brunswick. Atlantic Canada would have had to get the support of the government of Canada to reconstitute its economy and some of that work would have involved moving federal institutions out of Quebec and into the region."

In contrast with many of his ROC contemporaries, McKenna is not convinced that Canada or the federal government could have truly prepared for a Yes vote. He argues that the very act of undergoing such preparations would have enhanced the credibility of the sovereignist case in Quebec and the legitimacy of the referendum outside Quebec.

But he does wonder whether it might not have been better over the long run for Canada if his side had narrowly lost the 1995 referendum. "There are times in my heart of hearts when I wish they had won the referendum because I think it would have been the end of this issue for a lifetime . . . If the referendum had gone the other way it would have been obvious within a matter of days that Quebec was like a dog chasing the car and not knowing what to do with the car once it catches it," he predicts.

He thinks a close victory would have backfired on the sovereignist winners and damaged their cause beyond repair. "You would have a Quebec with no counter-party to negotiate with [in Canada]. You would have a Canada that would see a very dramatic reaction in terms of currency, in terms of credit rating. I don't think the people in Quebec appreciated the intensity of the reaction in the rest of Canada. You'd get a lot of pressure to do things like take the Quebec mandate out of Air Canada, VIA Rail, CN Rail . . . They would be moved out of there; military bases would be shut down. So many things would get triggered very quickly, starting with the divisibility issue. The debate over partition would have reared its head. You'd get a certain amount of buyer's remorse. A certain amount of people would have said: What have we done? What does this really mean?"

As of his first days as premier in 1987, Frank McKenna had been an active constitutional player, pressing for changes to the Meech Lake Accord until he finally put the deal, along with a side agreement addressing some of his concerns, to the New Brunswick legislature for ratification three years later and then taking part in the Charlottetown round. But the night of October 30, 1995, marked the beginning of the end of Frank McKenna's spell in the unity trenches. He resigned as premier two years later.

Jean Chrétien subsequently tried to entice him into running for a seat in Parliament and taking on a senior cabinet position—an offer he considered and eventually declined.

After Chrétien retired, McKenna served as Paul Martin's envoy to Washington, and when the latter resigned in 2006 the former New Brunswick premier was assiduously courted to run for the Liberal leadership. But in the end he resisted those siren calls. As coveted a political property as the former premier had been, the final week of the referendum campaign brought McKenna as close to the federal arena as he would ever come.

CHAPTER 16

A MAN FOR ALL SEASONS: BOB RAE

By the last week of the referendum campaign the federalist camp was awash with speculation about the morning after a sovereignist victory. Talk of a "unity cabinet" to anchor Prime Minister Jean Chrétien's authority filled the backrooms of the No camp.

Tory leader Jean Charest got a whiff of Chrétien's plan and of a list-in-the-making of potential participants from his sources around Parliament Hill. Charest still had a fair amount of backdoor access to the corridors of federal power; it had only been two years since he had lost his status as a government insider. He was one of only two Tory MPs, but still commanded a sizeable and well-connected contingent in the Senate—and voices within those various connections kept repeating one name.

"I had heard about a plan to set up a coalition government that I would presumably have been part of. But Bob Rae's name also came up repeatedly. Some felt that he, as a bilingual former premier, had the kind of national profile to act as a bridge between Ontario, Quebec and the New Democrats across Canada."

Rae himself says he was never formally approached for a post-Yes role. But he stops well short of ruling out the possibility that he would have been asked. "No one talked to me about what-if scenarios. The prime minister and I never discussed it. It may well have been, but I was not aware of it."

Rae's response jibes with Charest's sense that if the prime minister had backup plans to address any possible post-referendum needs, very few people would know until it was clear those plans would be needed.

In the lead-up to the vote, news that the federal government was preparing for a federalist defeat would truly have devastated the already declining morale of the No side. It would also have provided Chrétien's foes—inside and outside the sovereignist camp—with some precious post-referendum ammunition. There was also the risk that some Quebec voters—made aware that the federal government would respond to a pro-sovereignty vote by bending over backwards to keep their province within the federation—would vote yes to send a strong message of discontent to the rest of the country. And should the federalist side avoid a referendum defeat, knowledge of a strategy to develop a coalition government or any other contingency plan would just highlight Chrétien's political vulnerability. Win or lose, the prime minister's post-vote position was bound to be fragile.

By the end of the campaign, polls suggested that if the federalist option prevailed, it would be by an uncomfortably small margin. On the morning after a narrow No vote, the federal government would not be out of the woods. It would have to be accountable to a stunned Canadian electorate for having come so close to defeat. Pointed questions would be directed at the prime minister. The opposition parties would feel more than justified having a field day in question period. The government would also have to put its (exhausted) mind to the task of avoiding a risky referendum rematch. Chrétien had no interest in showing his post-Yes hand before he was forced to play it.

But if things did take a turn for the worse on referendum night, there was no doubt that (a) the prime minister could count on Rae; and (b) the former premier's services would be needed.

Like Frank McKenna, Bob Rae had a good rapport with Jean Chrétien. In 1995 Rae had yet to leave the NDP for the Liberal Party, but the prime minister and the former Ontario premier already had strong personal ties. Rae's brother, John, had helped mastermind Chrétien's rise to the Liberal leadership and, subsequently, to the pinnacle of federal power.

Moreover, in the lead-up to the referendum campaign, Bob Rae had personally made the pitch to Chrétien that he should not consider throwing in the towel if he lost. "I had a number of conversations with Mr. Chrétien after he was elected and spent a great deal of time talking with him about the fact that whatever happened, we had to keep the country together. I never believed that a 50 percent plus 1 vote in Quebec would have necessarily meant the independence of Quebec. I always believed that there were a lot of things that you needed to think about, on a go-forward basis as to how you would deal with that, how you would manage it."

It was a point that Rae had continued to hammer home even after he was no longer a premier. In the summer of

1995, a few months after the defeat of his NDP government in Ontario, he had visited the prime minister's official summer residence at Harrington Lake. As Rae recalls, that was their last real conversation about the upcoming referendum. Despite the prime minister's public demeanour of absolute confidence in a federalist victory, it seems that the scenario of a defeat came up for discussion.

"I talked about how his job as prime minister was to keep the country together and how that had to be crystal clear. I reminded him that the way the referendum was built, no one could assume that the country was finished, that the question did not lend itself to that inevitable conclusion."

That summer most federalists in and outside Quebec believed that the referendum would be a walk in the park. Rae was not one of them, and his less-than-rosy forecast was based on intimate knowledge of the dynamics that had led Canada and Quebec to the referendum crossroads.

"It is hard now for people to appreciate the extent to which at that time the question of the country, the future of the country and Quebec's place in it, was a central preoccupation. For that whole part of my political life it was a central preoccupation, whether it was as an MP or a leader of the opposition [at Queen's Park] or as premier. It was a major preoccupation."

Rae had become Ontario premier in the fall of 1990 in the midst of a constitutional crisis. "The issue of the failure of Meech was everywhere. Premier Bourassa was very ill. The premiers were not talking to each other. Brian Mulroney was in a deep funk, totally understandably. Support for independence in Quebec was upward of 60 percent. I knew that during the entire time that I was in government that was going to be a central issue. Trying to bring the temperature down again and bringing things back on the rails."

Throughout the first part of his rocky mandate in provincial power, Bob Rae carried a full constitutional load at the first ministers' table. He was a leading architect of the 1992 Charlottetown Accord and, although it barely passed muster in Ontario and was soundly rejected nationally, he still believes it was worth the time and effort that he and his fellow premiers put into negotiating it.

"Part of the purpose of the Charlottetown process was to simply prevent the worst of alternatives [a Quebec referendum on sovereignty] from coming up too quickly and doing everything we could to persuade the country and Quebecers that we were still serious about the possibility of constitutional reform. It did not succeed, but there is no way of knowing whether, if we had not made the effort, things might not have gone off the rails more quickly."

His constitutional efforts had raised Rae's profile in Quebec and made him some friends—most notably No camp leader Daniel Johnson. While other non-Quebec politicians were kept at bay by the No camp or, as in the case of Sheila Copps, put on make-work projects where they could do no harm, Rae had a front-row seat on the main campaign tour.

At Johnson's invitation, Rae actually spent time on the No bus. On a number of occasions he delivered the opening act to Johnson's stump speech, introducing the leader of Quebec's federalist forces. "We had become good friends while we were both premiers," says Rae, to explain why he was welcome on the No campaign.

As Rae travelled the province with Johnson, the subdued federalist mood that he encountered confirmed his pre-referendum fears. "The concern I had all the way through was that our crowds were loyal and supportive but older and smaller. This had been a concern I had in Quebec when I first campaigned in 1980 [for the first referendum]. Back then they [the No camp] kept saying: we would like you to go in this seniors' home to make a speech, and I would say: we've got to engage in the colleges, develop some arguments to stir things up a bit. And they would say: no, no, no. I'd always been worried about that generational issue."

On the ground, the wind that the No camp believed it had at its back was elusive. Rae had long worried about the wide-spread presumption of the federalist forces that victory was theirs for the taking. It was not long before events proved him right. "There was some overconfidence which concerned me. The feeling was that as long as Parizeau was there, he could always be managed because there was a ceiling of support for the kind of approach that he took. But what we saw in the campaign was that as soon as you took him out of the picture and put Bouchard back in, the whole thing was transformed."

By the morning of October 30, Bob Rae was bracing for a Yes vote. But he still did not subscribe to the notion that it should pave the way straight to the negotiation of Quebec's departure. Instead he was ready to take on the sovereignist movement on a much larger stage. "I thought the prime minister would have to say to Canadians that the country is not going to break up. There is no basis in this referendum upon which to break up the country. There is no mandate here for independence in international law or otherwise. That is the way we have to go.

"I certainly anticipated that we would be in a period of tremendous uncertainty; that Parizeau would appeal to the French to recognize Quebec. We'd be fighting at the United Nations, we would be fighting in every forum."

There is no doubt that if Jean Chrétien set out to appeal and eventually reverse a pro-sovereignty verdict—a task for which Rae had repeatedly encouraged him to prepare—he would be in sore need of the services of the former Ontario premier, and not just as a friendly sounding board.

For sure, the odds were that Jean Charest would not accept a narrow Yes vote at face value; that was his natural inclination, as the briefing notes prepared for him in anticipation of a possible narrow Yes vote and his own words suggest. Daniel Johnson was also predisposed to resist the proposition that a close sovereignist victory put Quebec on the fast track to independence. And ministers such as Paul Martin and André Ouellet made no secret of their willingness to resist a Yes vote at all costs.

But Charest's party had been all but wiped out in the previous election. His last regiment on Parliament Hill was mostly made up of unelected senators. As for Johnson, after a Yes vote his days as leader of the Quebec Liberal Party were likely numbered. And even if he hung on to his post, the party stood to be riddled by internal divisions and defections.

And then Chrétien did not have much of a personal rapport with most of his No allies. At one time or another they had all seen him as part of Quebec's problem rather than part of the country's solution. The prime minister's relationship with Charest, Johnson, Martin and Ouellet was based on necessity, not trust. More importantly, they were all Quebecers who, like Chrétien, would bear the brunt of the blame for having failed to persuade their province to remain in the Canadian fold.

If the federalists lost the referendum, Chrétien and his government would have to fend off a sovereignist offensive at home and on the international stage. But even to maintain itself in power, the Liberal government would have to fight on a number of other fronts, starting with the House of Commons where the Reform Party awaited its opportunity to make the Liberals pay for their failure in Quebec. As it happens, Bob Rae was well positioned on several of those fronts to help the beleaguered prime minister.

To have a hope of leading an undivided Canada out of the quagmire of a Yes vote, Jean Chrétien would have needed to maintain a minimal level of social peace. That would have involved immediately calming the fears of Quebec's First

Nations. They were adamantly opposed to Quebec's bid for independence and insisted that their territories should and could remain under Canadian jurisdiction. Short of that, some did not rule out full-fledged independence of their own. On October 30, their answer to the referendum question was a massive No, with nations such as the Cree rejecting sovereignty in a proportion higher than 90 percent.

It would have been an understatement to describe the question of Quebec's territorial integrity as sensitive. It bordered on explosive. The potential for civil strife was real and high. In the summer of 1990 an armed standoff between the Mohawk community at Oka, Quebec, and the Quebec provincial police had resulted in the seventy-eight-day blockade of a bridge leading to the island of Montreal. The Canadian military was eventually called in to bring the confrontation to an end.

Over the same period, the Cree in northern Quebec had fought and won an international public relations battle against the Great Whale hydro development project, forcing Hydro-Québec to beat a retreat and shelve its plan. After the election of the Parti Québécois, Matthew Coon Come—the Cree grand chief—had served notice that his nation would not go along with Quebec secession. Premier Parizeau might have been convinced that the accord the province had struck with the Cree at the time of the James Bay hydro development precluded that option, but his First Nations interlocutors begged to differ. A few days before the province-wide referendum the Cree had held one of their own, with 96 percent voting in support of separating from an independent Quebec.

In an interview given a year before the referendum, federal Indian Affairs minister Ron Irwin had caused a stir when he stated that by virtue of their right to self-determination, Quebec's First Nations had the right to choose to stay with Canada along with their territory.

Bob Rae was considered a friend in good standing by many First Nations leaders. As premier at the time of the Charlottetown constitutional round he had championed their demands. Unlike most politicians on either side of the Quebec/Canada debate, he could count on an attentive audience in the country's aboriginal communities. No one in Jean Chrétien's cabinet—including Minister Irwin—could count on the same level of First Nations trust.

Chrétien's party had solid support in Atlantic Canada. The same was not true of Western Canada, where the Liberals were chronically weak but Rae's New Democrat associates had a lot more presence. In 1995, Alberta, most of rural British Columbia and significant sections of Saskatchewan and Manitoba were solid Reform territory. But provincially the NDP was in power in British Columbia and Saskatchewan, and it was a force to contend with in Manitoba. For many New Democrats the prospect of living in a Canada ruled by the socially conservative Reform Party was almost as daunting—if not more—than a Canada without Quebec. Rae—still a lifelong New Democrat—had connections with the political forces most likely to offer Chrétien a counter-weight to Manning and his troops in Western Canada. (On that score the prime minister would also have sorely needed his old friend Roy Romanow in his national unity cabinet.)

In Chrétien's battle to survive a Reform challenge, Ontario's newly elected Progressive Conservative premier also would have played a pivotal role. Mike Harris and Jean Chrétien did not know each other well and they had precious little in common, politically or otherwise. But they shared a common political base—and among that base Harris had just beaten Rae and his New Democrats out of office. More popular in Quebec than Ontario, Rae was *persona non grata* with much of his province's electorate. And on just about every provincial issue, Rae saw white where Harris saw black and vice versa.

Still Rae had helped draft the main speech that Mike Harris repeatedly delivered over the course of the referendum campaign and the new premier had a lot of time for his predecessor's constitutional savvy. He almost certainly trusted his instincts on that score more than he trusted Preston Manning's. There is little doubt that Rae's advice would have influenced or at least informed the post-Yes thinking of the Ontario premier.

If the Yes had prevailed on October 30, 1995, no one seriously believes that Bob Rae would have gone home to watch the action from the relative comfort of his forced political retirement. With dark clouds gathering on Chrétien's horizon in Ontario, in Western Canada, on the aboriginal front and in the House of Commons, Rae would not have walked away from the very battle to which he had long ago urged on the prime minister, before a sovereignist victory was really in the cards. As he would prove in the years to come, Rae was hardly done with politics after his Ontario defeat, although provincial and NDP politics were essentially done with him.

The federalist referendum victory did not completely clear Chrétien's sky, but it did push back enough clouds to give the prime minister a chance to get his government out of the rain. Still, even with a referendum victory accomplished, Rae did not go home. Instead, he became a vocal behind-the-scenes advocate of the federal Liberals' Clarity Act.

Rae says he came around to the need for the law even before his side almost lost to the Yes vote. "In my conversations with Chrétien leading to the referendum, I argued that there had to be a better way of doing this and a better plan and a better approach than this going after each other. Let's establish some rules of the game; let's understand what is going on here; let's understand that you can't just say that you got a Yes to a mushy question and now you are gone. That is not going to work. It is not a tenable position. In the absence of an agreement on what the rules are, you then have to say: here are the rules that will guide our response."

Against most expectations, the unity issue slowly but surely faded from the centre of the national radar over the two decades that followed the referendum. Bob Rae still could not stay home. Instead he reinvented himself as a federal Liberal and set his sites on leadership of the party.

By his own words his political life had largely been defined by the unity issue. It could be that as the issue faded, so did the opportunity to realize his dream of becoming prime minister. Thinking back to the political storm that would have resulted from a federalist defeat in the Quebec referendum makes clear that Rae's services would have been more essential to his country in November 1995 than they were in more recent years, when he tried so hard to become one of Jean Chrétien's successors.

A final note: It is rare that a politician errs on the side of modesty—especially when looking in the rear-view mirror—but as he talks about his time in the federalist trenches in Quebec, Rae underplays his impact on that province. Quebecers' esteem for him survived both his demise as Ontario premier and the travails of the referendum campaign.

Eleven years after the Quebec vote, Rae joined Michael Ignatieff and Stéphane Dion in the first tier of candidates to succeed Paul Martin as Liberal leader. Back then Prime Minister Stephen Harper had not yet been in power for a full year, but Quebecers were already starting to sour on his Conservative government. Stéphane Dion was the Quebec native son in the Liberal lineup, but that could not make up for the heavy baggage that he carried in his home province. At the behest of Jean Chrétien, Dion had played the leading role in the crafting of the Clarity Act, and many Quebecers never forgot—or forgave—his doing so.

Michael Ignatieff, on the other hand, was a fresh face with the kind of public intellectual credentials that can amount to a good calling card with Quebec voters. He had distinguished himself by jumping to the front of the federal parade to formally recognize Quebec as a nation. That did not play well with many Liberals, but it was a move that Harper embraced. Taking advantage of Ignatieff's support, the prime minister had a motion on the Quebec nation concept passed in the House of Commons in the middle of the Liberal leadership campaign.

Over the rather tumultuous months of the 2006 leadership race and against the backdrop of the Quebec nation debate on Parliament Hill, I would routinely quiz my francophone dinner guests about which Liberal horse they liked best. If voting Liberal could ensure a Conservative defeat in the next election, was there a candidate in the lineup for whom they might abandon the Bloc Québécois?

Dion never surfaced as an option—a result that did not surprise me, given his poor standing with many francophone voters—but then Ignatieff elicited at best only lukewarm support. Had they been Liberal Party members, most of my dinner guests would have supported Bob Rae for leader.

When I asked them why they would pass over Ignatieff— the Liberal godfather of the Quebec nation resolution—they answered that the nation business was mostly semantics. Rae, however, was a superior choice because as a former New Democrat he had demonstrated real social democrat credentials. In hindsight, those conversations and the craving they brought to the surface for a clearly progressive federalist option on the federal ballot were a harbinger of Quebec's next great political surprise—the orange wave that resulted in an NDP sweep of its francophone ridings five years later.

PART 5

THE LAST WORD

CHAPTER 17

THE CONJURER: JEAN CHRÉTIEN

In the saga of the 1995 referendum, all roads inevitably lead back to Jean Chrétien . . . and to a barrage of smoke. Those who know the former prime minister will not be surprised that two decades after the fact he still insists on keeping his post-referendum cards close to his chest. Or that he says he did not think out all his possible moves ahead of the vote.

"I had a number of cards that I ended up not having to play. I do not like to discuss them. There would have been quite a number of options at my disposal in the event of a Yes vote. But I wasted no time on them. That would have been for later if needed."

A veil of silence obscures our view for only so long. No fabric is immune to the wear and tear brought on by time and so it is with the cloak in which Jean Chrétien continues to wrap himself and his contingency plans.

Based on the referendum recollections of the federalists interviewed for this book, one could be forgiven for thinking that the prime minister had a stand-in speaking by rote

on stage while the real Chrétien watched, plotted and ago-
nized from behind the curtain. The insouciant Jean Chrétien
who brushes off Preston Manning's calls for a different referendum approach, and is deaf to similar appeals from a
friend and ally such as Roy Romanow, sounds strikingly
different from the one who uses slang to discuss his referendum angst with his nephew in Washington.

The prime minister who for so long was content to tell
Canadians that all is going well in Quebec does not come
across as the same person who, even before the Quebec
campaign started or the polls soured for his side, was discussing the aftermath of a possible federalist defeat with Bob
Rae at Harrington Lake.

The Chrétien who keeps his cabinet in the dark about
his morning-after plans and frowns at the idea that his officials would spend time drafting such plans is hard to reconcile with the one who phones Premier Frank McKenna to
ask if he will join a national unity cabinet.

Among the federalist politicians we talked to, it was
those in closest contact with the prime minister—Bob Rae,
Frank McKenna, Raymond Chrétien—who were most
convinced on the morning of the referendum that they
should brace for the worst.

In Chrétien's own interview, I encountered predictably
more of the happy-go-lucky persona that he so likes to present to the world and less of the introspective political animal
that he really is. To see evidence of the true conjurer at
work, one must take stock of the gap between his public
words and his private interactions.

Today for instance, Jean Chrétien glibly claims that he personally would have done well after a Yes vote. "I used to tell people that they did not need to worry about my fate if Quebec seceded. I would tell them that I would buy a nice cheap house in Westmount, open a big law office downtown and anyone in the rest of Canada who would have needed to do business with Quebec would have called on my services. Because a sovereign Quebec would have needed to have links with the rest of Canada, and as someone who had one foot on each side, I would have been the best person to hire. I used to say: if Quebec separates don't worry about me, I will be flush with money."

But on the night of the referendum the prime minister's mood was not so light. His body language at the time of his last campaign speech in Verdun and on the night of the vote itself fooled no one, least of all his fellow Quebecers. He looked like a ghost of his usual, confident self. Chrétien went live on national television late on October 30 and, although the federalists did not lose the vote, he looked as shaken as Canadians had ever seen him.

Shortly after the Quebec referendum a home invasion at 24 Sussex Drive rattled him further. Over the same period, he conducted a failed meeting with Ontario premier Mike Harris in a manner that oozes more post-traumatic stress than political foresight. It would take some time for the old Chrétien to return.

In February 1996, Chrétien (briefly) throttled an anti-poverty demonstrator at an event in Gatineau, Quebec. The fact that his impulsive gesture played to rave reviews in many Canadian quarters must have told him something not only about the state of his own nerves but also about the hardened post-referendum mindset of the country. It must have confirmed his worst fears about the backlash that would have attended a Quebec Yes vote, but also boosted his confidence that he could get back in the country's good books despite what was widely criticized as a lacklustre referendum performance.

Handed a Yes vote, Chrétien would have seen his options essentially boiled down to two—neither of which was guaranteed to help Canada or Quebec arrive at a mutually satisfying resolution to the crisis.

He could attempt to slow the Yes train down long enough that he could try to switch it onto another track, one that led to a destination other than the break-up of Canada; or, failing that, long enough to sketch out a roadmap to guide Canada and Quebec through uncharted constitutional territory; or, if all else failed, long enough to hand the controls of a functioning federal government to someone else. In theory, as prime minister, Chrétien was in the driver's seat. But no one—starting with him—could anticipate how quickly the acid of a Yes vote would corrode the lines that connected him to the political gears driving the federal government.

The alternative was to accept responsibility for the defeat on that night, resign and let events take their course without him. Under that scenario, the other Quebecers who occupied key positions in his government would presumably have been morally obliged to follow suit. Quebec MPs such as Paul Martin at finance and André Ouellet at foreign affairs would have had to take Chrétien's cue and leave the scene.

But departures might not have stopped there. In 1995 the Quebec presence at the top of the federal pyramid extended far beyond the elected politicians who made up the Liberal government. The Clerk of the Privy Council, Jocelyne Bourgon, was a Quebecer and she ran the federal public service. Antonio Lamer, the Chief Justice of the Supreme Court, was also from Quebec, as were scores of other ambassadors besides Raymond Chrétien in Washington. After a Yes, all those roles would have had strategic importance.

Faced with a hemorrhage of Quebec blood, the ROC politicians who would have inherited the leadership of the government would have had to contend with a sudden and unprecedented vacuum at the top, and it would be happening at the most uncertain hour in Canada's history.

Jean Chrétien will not discuss what tentative conclusions he reached as he contemplated the way forward after a federalist defeat. If he had his way, he would have you believe that he hadn't troubled himself to reach any. His call to McKenna about a national unity cabinet suggests otherwise. It also suggests that in the face of a narrow Yes vote he would not have given up his job or conceded defeat for federalism without a fight.

On Chrétien's watch, what was good for the Liberal Party in Quebec was routinely considered to be good for the country. On that basis, the former prime minister once described showering Liberal-friendly Quebec ridings (including his own) with job-creation money as part of a day's work on behalf of Canadian unity. That rationale would never have been as central to his thinking as on the morning after a Yes vote, when keeping Canada together and keeping himself in power would have gone hand-in-hand for Jean Chrétien.

The other seventeen men and women we interviewed for this book had very different and sometimes conflicting perspectives on the post-Yes federal environment. But to some of them, every possible outcome following a Yes vote would lead to asking whether Chrétien's leadership of the country and the government should survive. That was particularly true of the ROC politicians, regardless of their partisan affiliation or the level of government that they represented.

The leaders of the sovereignist camp agreed on little else, but they concurred that the odds were low of Jean Chrétien surviving a defeat. Over on the other side, his own nephew, Raymond, also thought his uncle's days as prime minister (as well as his own days as ambassador) might be numbered.

Jean Chrétien agrees that there was a real possibility that a Yes vote would have terminated his political career. He does not rule out that he could have resigned after a referendum defeat, but not right away and possibly not unless he was under great pressure to do so.

"I might have decided that it was a personal defeat. I might have washed my hands of the entire affair and quit. But I don't give up easily and quitting is not in my nature. I certainly would not have resigned the next day and said: 'Vive le Québec libre.' That would not have happened."

On the issue of the legitimacy of his Liberal government after a Yes vote, Chrétien is even more categorical: "I was a francophone prime minister, but I held ninety-eight of ninety-nine Ontario seats. No one was more legitimate than I was. My base was not in Quebec, where I had twenty MPs. I was prime minister because of Ontario, because of Atlantic Canada, and I even held seats in Alberta."

Reform Party leader Preston Manning has suggested that his MPs would have walked out of Parliament if Chrétien stonewalled his calls for a post-Yes federal election. The former prime minister maintains that he could have continued to govern in the absence of the leading federalist opposition party: "If the Reform had left the House, I would have had an easier time. You are legitimate until you quit. Manning might have dreamt of becoming prime minister once Quebec was gone. But I had a majority government. It would have been a big battle that I am just as happy to have avoided."

Brian Tobin—as a former member of Chrétien's ministerial team—contends that there would have needed to be a swift rebalancing of the cabinet in favour of non-Quebec ministers like himself. Chrétien does not disagree that his ROC ministers could have made his life difficult. But he believes their pre-vote deliberations had more to do with a bad case of nerves than a serious plan to curtail his political discretion.

"I heard about their meeting. It did not concern me. Had they all resigned, it would have been another matter. I too was not happy when I saw the polls in the last week of the campaign. I too worried."

On the more specific issue of the chain of events set in motion by a Yes vote and the prospect of secession negotiations, he is convinced that with or without him in the picture, the issue of Quebec partition would have quickly surfaced under the impetus of the Quebec aboriginal people. "The First Nations have a large capital of sympathy. It would have been difficult for Quebec to say we do not respect the popular will of the First Nations to remain with Canada."

Lucien Bouchard, Mario Dumont and Roy Romanow, among others, anticipated or feared that in the face of a federal refusal to engage in secession talks Jacques Parizeau would quickly proceed to his Plan B: a unilateral declaration of Quebec's independence. Paul Martin, Brian Tobin and Raymond Chrétien said the possibility of a Quebec UDI was one of the few scenarios that the federal government had actually discussed and tried to prepare for.

For his part, Jean Chrétien is convinced that Canada would not have lacked for international help to fend off a Quebec bid for de facto international recognition. "What would other countries have done? They all had their own problems with national minorities. Before taking on Canada, they would have thought twice. Even the French would have."

As for the campaign itself and the unexpectedly dangerous turn that it took in its final weeks, Chrétien readily admits that it was his call to not have officials work on contingency plans for a federal loss. "In 1980 a committee had worked on contingency plans. I had refused to see them. I was not interested in negative scenarios. I had a job to do and it was to win the referendum. I had told Trudeau as much."

The former prime minister remains convinced that he would have won the referendum hands down, except for two interconnected developments. The recasting of Lucien Bouchard as the star of the No campaign was one. "Before Bouchard came in, we were leading by twenty points. It turned the campaign around. When one campaigns with a cane, it works," says Chrétien—a clear reference to the late NDP leader Jack Layton, who was visibly ailing during the 2011 federal election campaign that saw his party sweep Quebec.

Chrétien argues that the combination of Bouchard's appeal with a profoundly ambiguous referendum question made for an almost irresistible mix. "Even I could perhaps have voted yes to such a question. People would tell me: I don't want to separate but I want a new deal. For many, the question meant that Lucien Bouchard would negotiate a better deal for Quebecers, one that might even free them from paying taxes to the federal government."

Jean Chrétien is anything but the kind of political retiree who wears regrets on his sleeve. If anything, he is predisposed to blow his own horn. But if he were to second-guess his handling of the 1995 referendum, it sounds as if it would be specifically on the matter of the question. "I had always believed that the question was a big problem. At eighty-five words, it was long and confusing."

In fact, Chrétien initially fought hard behind the scenes to place the referendum question under a microscope. A federal committee even drafted a text to dissect it line by line and to poke holes into the notion that Quebecers were voting for a future partnership with Canada rather than for separation. The prime minister wanted that text sent to every Quebec household above his and Daniel Johnson's signature. Chrétien's Quebec lieutenant, André Ouellet, says the Quebec Liberals took weeks to respond to the federal proposal. At some point Chrétien lost patience and threatened to do it without them. But he backed off when the Quebec No committee eventually offered to produce an annotated version of the PQ's draft bill on sovereignty to highlight the fact that, with or without a partnership, Quebec would separate after a Yes victory. According to Ouellet, the document that resulted from the compromise between the prime minister and the Johnson camp was never widely circulated.

Many of the federal and non-Quebec politicians we interviewed shared frustration at having been kept at bay by the Quebec No camp. Jean Chrétien acknowledges the awkwardness of a referendum structure that is deliberately designed to revolve strictly around the National Assembly and the provincial political arena. "The difficulty is that the leader of the No camp is the leader of the opposition in the National Assembly, while the real adversary is the prime minister. So you are in but you are still on the sidelines."

As it happens, the 1995 Yes camp struggled with the same challenge when it realized that the referendum rules consigned Lucien Bouchard—by far its best salesman—to the back of the store in the House of Commons. The Parti Québécois, when it crafted a referendum bill in the late seventies, had not foreseen the advent of a federal sovereignist party or of a federal sovereignist leader more popular than the sitting premier. There was no role written in the Quebec act for a federal figure such as Bouchard. It had to be invented on the fly, in the heat of the action.

But while the sovereignist forces eagerly rallied behind the leader of the Bloc Québécois, and in many instances had long been calling for Bouchard's ascent, any parallel attempt to substitute Jean Chrétien for Daniel Johnson would have led to disaster. For many francophone federalists, a prime minister whom they closely associated with both the controversial patriation episode and the demise of the Meech Lake Accord was a liability, not an asset.

At least initially, Jean Chrétien had to settle for the place that Pierre Trudeau had carved out for himself during the first referendum. "I decided to make three speeches; that was exactly the number that Pierre Trudeau delivered in 1980. I'm a fighter. I might have liked to do more but I accepted the rationale that I should stick to Trudeau's pattern."

In the last of those three speeches, Jean Chrétien reversed himself on the issue of the constitutional recognition of Quebec's distinct society, a concept that had no more influential critic than Pierre Trudeau. Chrétien says that, just prior to the vote, he gave his predecessor a heads-up about his reversal.

"Before I promised to do something about the distinct society I called Trudeau. I did not want him to contradict me in public. He told me: you're the boss; do what you want. The conflict I had with Trudeau over distinct society was that I thought it was meaningless and I did not see the point of fighting against it. At some point, I told myself: if that is what Quebecers want so much, let's just do it."

It was not the first time that Chrétien pleaded with Trudeau to keep his peace on the distinct society issue, but it was the first time he succeeded.

During the Charlottetown Accord referendum in 1992, Chrétien, who was then the leader of the opposition, had tried to persuade Trudeau to tone down his opposition to enshrining the distinct society concept in the Constitution. "Trudeau and I had agreed to disagree. I had told him it was not worth making the issue a life-or-death one; that sometimes it was better to compromise. But Trudeau would not change his mind and it did give me problems with my caucus. We remained friends but his attitude did not help. Mind you, it did not prevent me from becoming prime minister."

Jean Chrétien won the 1995 referendum. But the result fell short of the decisive victory that would have put the sovereignty debate to rest. In hindsight, it may be that the sovereignist movement only exchanged the gift of a swift death for a slow but agonizing one. Since October 1995, polls suggest that one in five Yes supporters have changed their minds. The Parti Québécois has had four leaders since Jacques Parizeau resigned. Three of them—Lucien Bouchard, Bernard Landry and Pauline Marois—served as premier. None has managed to rekindle the sovereignist flame. As for the Bloc Québécois, it was relegated to the back of the House of Commons after its ranks were reduced to only four MPs in the 2011 election.

But in the immediate aftermath of the 1995 vote, the federalist picture did not look so rosy. After the referendum, Jean Chrétien invested a lot of energy and resources into changing the rules that would guide future federal governments in the event of another referendum. Instead of moving on to other policy fronts, he had to stand guard against a rematch in Quebec and, perhaps more importantly, he had to find ways to channel the referendum frustration of ROC voters at having been frozen out of the Quebec campaign into something other than a backlash against his Liberals.

Today Chrétien does not rule out that there could be one day another referendum, but he is satisfied that it will be fought under clearer rules of engagement. "They [the sovereignists] will not be able to ask another question like the 1995 one. It is intellectually honest to have a clear question. It was a mistake to try to win a mandate through the back door."

When we interviewed him for this book, Chrétien had been out of the game for a decade. There is no doubt that the steady decline in sovereignist fortunes since then encouraged him to diminish the harm to his career and his government that was nearly done by the bullet he so narrowly dodged.

When he looks back on his time in politics, it seems that the memories he most cherishes come from periods of great adversity. As prime minister, Jean Chrétien had to face not only a referendum that he nearly lost, he struggled with a dire fiscal crisis and the question of taking Canada to war in Iraq. Within his party, he contended with a civil war and an attempted putsch. One would think that after having fought all those battles he would be content to rest on his laurels. Instead he claims that he is sorry to have missed out on the challenge of running a minority government. He says it would have been "fun." Of the blood sport of politics, he remembers the thrill of battle rather than the pain of the effort.

Jean Chrétien loves to have the last word. For ten years, it was a privilege he enjoyed in his daily question period jousts with the leaders of the opposition. He used to talk about how he liked to twist a verbal knife into his opponents during his closing answer—when they could no longer strike back. It is logical that, of all the protagonists who generously agreed to relive the referendum drama for our benefit, he gets to speak at the end. Chances are that, for once, none of the others will take issue with his words. He might well be speaking for them all.

"What is politics? It is to skate on thin ice without ever knowing if it is about to open up, without ever knowing if you are on the verge of being sucked into the deep. You make one small mistake and you disappear and no one wants to see you anymore. Every day, you tell yourself that you have survived to live another day. That is the adrenaline of politics. To never know what will happen the next day makes for an exciting life!"

From that perspective, few nights in Canadian history were more exciting than the night of October 30, 1995.

AFTERWORD

SIZE MATTERS

In the hypothetical equation of a Yes vote in 1995, we face too many unknowns to offer a remotely valid estimate of how things would have played out. Juggling all the variables, we can come up with any number of contradictory scenarios.

Preston Manning said he would take a Yes vote as a green light to secession negotiations. Based on that interpretation, imagining, for instance, a Reform government teaming up with PQ premier Jacques Parizeau to usher Quebec out of Confederation would not be far-fetched. The mood in the rest of Canada after a federalist defeat could have shifted quickly enough from angst to anger and/or resignation and led to a Reform mandate to set the terms of Quebec's independence. That was certainly the direction of a strong undercurrent in public opinion at the time of the referendum campaign. From Jean Charest to Sheila Copps to Mike Harris and Brian Tobin, all those who spoke to us from the larger Canadian perspective alluded to it. At the tail end of the Meech Lake and Charlottetown rounds, the reservoir of constitutional goodwill between Quebec and the rest of Canada was already running dry. After a decade of talking at cross purposes, many voters in the rest of Canada, as in Quebec, had had it with what they saw as fruitless dialogue.

By all accounts Canada's business community would have followed a Yes vote by pushing hard for a process that restored as much certainty to the markets as possible on a timely basis. If following up on the referendum result with negotiations to hive Quebec out of the federation turned out to be the most effective way to achieve a return to relative stability, then that course of action would have had significant corporate support. Under that scenario, would Lucien Bouchard have found himself sitting across a table from Stephen Harper? The latter was then Manning's go-to MP on federal-provincial issues. It is not unlikely that he could have been the Reform's answer to Parizeau's lead negotiator. And in that case, which of the two—Bouchard or Harper—would have been the first to blink? The bets are open on that.

And what of André Ouellet's idea of a repeat referendum held under federal auspices? Would that have resulted, as Bernard Landry predicts, in a decisive pro-sovereignty mandate? Or would Quebecers have refused to vote yes to a question that more starkly put separation in the picture? Alternatively, what if that referendum had been about an offer of renewed federalism instead? Would other Canadians have supported such an offer or, as Premier Harris feared, would revisiting that poisoned well have led to an even more toxic result?

It is simple enough to draw a tentative line between a Yes vote and Jean Chrétien's ousting from office. Even he could imagine circumstances that would lead him to resign. But, initially at least, he would not have lacked support to stay on. It is clear that in the immediate aftermath of a Yes win Canada's political leadership would have been torn: some would have wanted to get on with redrawing the federation minus its francophone province; others would have wanted to stay in the trenches and fight a last-ditch battle to keep Quebec in. The ranks of the latter were not limited to Quebec-based politicians. They would have included dominant provincial figures such as Frank McKenna and, probably, Roy Romanow. The battle between those two ROC factions could have been as polarizing outside Quebec as the referendum debate had just been inside it.

It is equally plausible that differences over the meaning of a narrow victory could have brought the Yes camp to implosion. Mario Dumont for one was seeking a new federalist deal between his province and the rest of Canada, and Dumont's plan was an alternative to secession that Lucien Bouchard could have lived with. When he had first come to Parliament in 1988, the future leader of the Bloc was more interested in renewed federalism than incremental independence. Many Yes supporters were drawn to the sovereignist camp by the prospect of a different partnership with Canada more than by the prospect of Quebec's independence.

But what about the one third of Quebecers—like Jacques Parizeau—for whom sovereignty was and remains the only destination that makes it worth embarking on this voyage?

Would they really have accepted an interpretation of their Yes vote along federalist lines without a peep?

Also absent from the mix is the unpredictable sum of the individual reactions in Quebec and outside the province to what would have looked to many like a radical change in their citizenship . . . and their own lives.

Would a Yes vote have brought out the best or the worst in Canadians? Would reason have prevailed over emotion, as most of the protagonists on both sides suggested in their interviews? In the heat of the constitutional debates that led up to the Quebec referendum, reciprocal respect regularly gave way to over-the-top arguments. As often as not, fears based on perception, ignorance and/or outright prejudices rather than facts won the day. At the tail end of the Meech Lake debate, for instance, a number of women's associations (in the ROC) argued that the distinct society clause would allow a future Quebec government to coerce francophone women into having more children. On a stop in Winnipeg a few weeks before the end of the Meech Lake round, that notion was put to a parliamentary committee chaired by Jean Charest by a delegation of Manitoba women. It was a rare occasion when the Tory MP blew a gasket in public.

The context of past constitutional deliberations was not half as adversarial as the climate would have been in a post-Yes environment. In contrast to the Meech Lake and Charlottetown debates, the discussions would have involved fundamental issues of citizenship and day-to-day economics. It would have taken a while for cooler heads to prevail.

And one could hardly take for granted the capacity of the Canadian business and political establishment to lead public opinion toward mutually beneficial compromise. At the time of the federal referendum on the Charlottetown Accord, the persuasive powers of Canada's so-called opinion leaders turned out to be glaringly missing in action.

Given the self-imposed code of silence observed by much of the Canadian establishment on matters pertaining to the secession of Quebec, most voters would have had no reason to be prepared for the realities of a Yes victory. Many would have been angry not only at the Quebecers who had caused the crisis but also at those whom they would have held responsible for a rude awakening.

The fact that those—like Premier Roy Romanow or Reform leader Preston Manning—who tried to get Quebecers (and other Canadians) thinking about the consequences of a Yes vote were discouraged, speaks volume as to the strictness of that code of silence. It has relaxed somewhat since 1995. But on that score, it is ironic that Stephen Harper—who, as a Reform critic, was a vocal advocate of a more open, more frank Quebec/Canada conversation—has now as prime minister retreated behind his own wall of silence.

Put together any combination of the above ingredients and chances are the result will be off the mark. If anything is true in politics, it is that watershed events take on a life of their own and control over them quickly moves beyond the grasp of those who set them in motion.

Time and time again over the decades that I have covered Canadian politics, reality has exceeded the imaginative abilities of the finest political analysts. The past is not always a sound predictor of the future.

Think of Pierre Trudeau's 1980 resurrection as Canada's prime minister. He had resigned as Liberal leader after he lost the 1979 election and his party had not even have time to arrange a succession process before he was back in the saddle and in power for four transformative years. Or think again of the NDP orange wave that swept Quebec in the 2011 federal campaign. Based on all the available conventional wisdom, it—like a Yes vote in 1995—was simply not supposed to happen.

I was in Baie-Comeau for the triumphant Tory rally that Prime Minister Brian Mulroney held in November 1988 on the occasion of his second consecutive majority victory. No one in that room or anywhere else across the country that night would have imagined that only five years later Mulroney's Progressive Conservative Party—with him in political retirement—would be reduced to just two seats.

Who could have predicted that night that the Reform Party—a Western Canadian creation that was barely on the national radar and that had just failed to win a single seat—and the Bloc Québécois—a party that did not yet exist in the minds of its founders—would fill most of the opposition seats in the House of Commons only fifty-nine months later? If someone had suggested either change in the Canadian political landscape, he or she might have been gently led to a padded hospital room.

It was never our objective to impose an ordered narrative

on the inevitable chaos of the day after a Yes vote. Had we done that, you would have just read a novel. We were less interested in coming up with an approximate big picture than in preventing the ill-matched pieces of the referendum puzzle from being swept under the carpet of political history. They may not all fit together and form a coherent image of the day that almost was, but many of them have still found a place in the larger post-referendum political picture.

For instance, if one were to look for the genesis of Stephen Harper's rise to power, one could do worse than to parse the entrails of the 1995 referendum debate. He might have had no impact on the campaign in Quebec, but his frequent appearances on a variety of political panels did not go unnoticed in the backrooms of the rest of Canada. Unbound by the political correctness that prevented many non-Quebec politicians from speaking out of school about the possibility of a Yes vote, Harper's insights struck home with many in the voiceless political class of English-speaking Canada. He contended for instance that if Canada was divisible, Quebec was too. And in the immediate aftermath of the referendum, he argued in the House of Commons in May 1996 that if Quebec ever narrowly voted yes, other Canadians would let them go on terms favourable to the rest of the federation. "If the government of Quebec chooses to go into a negotiation in which it has 51 percent or 52 percent support, it puts itself into an extremely weak bargaining position with the rest of the country . . . It will bring Quebec to the table in a position where Quebecers are extremely weak and divided."

For the record, not just Conservatives told us that they felt Harper was a rare voice articulating key concerns on behalf of the ROC during that period. In 2011 Ontario voted with Western Canada to give Harper a majority (as of early 2014, he held 72 of the province's 106 seats). The near-death experience of the 1995 referendum undoubtedly increased the appeal of a prime minister such as Harper who is not beholden to Quebec for his or her power.

It is not always easy to draw a line between an essential critical distance and an unfairly judgmental approach. That is possibly even more of a challenge for commentators like the two of us who are usually expected to come down on one side or the other of an issue at very short notice. Anyone who has had to rate the performances of rival leaders on the night of an election debate knows the definition of coming up with a verdict under duress, at least in media terms.

When in doubt, we have tried to err on the side of letting our subjects speak for themselves rather than let our biases turn their words against them. We have also become much better listeners over the course of the year we spent interviewing the subjects of this book.

That being said, it is impossible to look at the 1995 political drama from the angle of a Yes victory without making a few observations. The main one from our perspective is that in such affairs as a referendum on independence size matters.

In 1995 most of the contradictions between players on the same side of either campaign, or between the rival sovereignist and the federalist camps, would have evaporated in the face of a conclusive Yes victory. Handed a 60 percent mandate, the leaders of the Yes camp would have had no hesitation in identifying the way forward. The grey zone within which Lucien Bouchard, Mario Dumont and Jacques Parizeau seemed headed for a showdown would not have existed. A strong Yes showing would also have dissipated most of the post-vote fog that to this day envelops the No side. The Quebecers who had fought for the losing federalist side in Quebec and in Ottawa would have not only taken note of the result but (regretfully) would have had to endorse it and move on from their pan-Canadian roles. Their peers from the ROC would have, as Brian Tobin put it, taken over their responsibilities.

It is possible that the conditions for a strong pro-sovereignty mandate will never be recreated. That proposition fuels both the attachment of so many in the sovereignist movement to the simple 50-plus-1 majority rule and the push by many on the other side of the debate to insist on a higher threshold.

The same people who—if they were union leaders—would be reluctant to have workers walk out on the basis of a split strike vote for fear of leading them in an impoverishing and losing battle would apparently—on the same fragile basis—not hesitate to embark on a secession negotiation with Canada that would impact the daily lives of millions of their fellow citizens.

But for all the talk in federalist circles about the setting of a higher bar for a decisive Yes vote, the fact that no one has come up with another number that inspires a minimum amount of consensual support says all that needs to be said about the difficulty of finding an acceptable alternative. Unilaterally setting a higher threshold for a sovereignty vote from the heights of Parliament Hill would still leave the riddle of what to make of a simple majority Yes vote unsolved. In practical terms, it would be impossible to go on as if nothing had happened on the morning after. The sovereignist side—speaking as it would for more Quebecers than at any other time in its history—certainly would not. At the end of the day, Stephen Harper's argument (circa 1996) remains valid: a narrow Yes victory would essentially be a problem for the sovereignists and an asset to ROC negotiators in any subsequent talks on the terms of secession.

As for the contention of some federalist tenors that raising the bar for a successful Yes vote would basically ensure that there would never be another Quebec referendum on sovereignty, it should be noted that there was a time—not that far removed from the 1995 vote—when close to two-thirds of Quebecers would have given their government a mandate to part the province from the federation.

In the weeks and months after the June 1990 failure of the Meech Lake Constitutional Accord, Quebecers' support for sovereignty skyrocketed. Then-premier Robert Bourassa— otherwise a lifelong federalist—promised that in the absence of an acceptable constitutional "offer" from the rest of Canada, he would put the question of their political future to Quebecers in a referendum to be held no later than the fall of 1992.

It could be that Bourassa was just killing time, that he was playing with the rest of the country's nerves in the hope for a better constitutional deal and in the expectation that

Quebec's bout of nationalist fever would abate. Bob Rae, who worked closely with Bourassa over the period between Meech Lake and Charlottetown, thinks as much. The former Ontario premier had argued that the time spent on negotiating the Charlottetown Accord was well spent even if in the end the deal was rejected. He believes that it at least allowed emotions, on both sides, to die down. Frank McKenna, for his part, says he borrowed one of the lines for what would have been his speech in the event of a Yes victory from Bourassa. "After the demise of Meech I was quite disconsolate at the prospect of its consequences and he said, 'The Latin blood is boiling right now. Let it cool down and we will start talking again . . .'"

In a previous journalistic life, former Parti Québécois minister Jean-François Lisée wrote two books that add up to a compelling case that Bourassa never meant to follow through on his referendum commitment. But a more human element could account at least in part for Bourassa's disorderly retreat from his post-Meech promise. Shortly after Meech Lake failed, Bourassa was handed a life-threatening cancer diagnosis. That would have impacted any thought about putting the issue of their political future to Quebecers, knowing as he then did that he might not be around to manage the aftermath of the vote and the monumental task that would have resulted from a Yes victory.

A number of our federalist interviewees—notably former prime minister Jean Chrétien—have argued that Lucien Bouchard's episode of flesh-eating disease in 1994, and the subsequent loss of a leg, led to his swift elevation to political sainthood, a status that put him out of reach of the attacks of mere political humans. Since the 2011 NDP sweep of Quebec, some of the same people have suggested as much about late leader Jack Layton. But at the end of the day the argument is more reductive than persuasive. Its main merit is to spare those who advance it the task of looking at themselves in the mirror and facing the reasons for their own relative lack of success. It also spares them from having to spend too much time accounting for the uncomfortable reality that—as they demonstrated in 1995 but also in 2011—Quebecers are collectively capable of charting a new course at a political moment's notice.

For the record, it is far from certain that if Prime Minister Stephen Harper were unfortunate enough to have to face down a major health challenge he would subsequently lead his Conservatives to a winning Quebec score in the following federal election. But those who insist on clinging to the thesis that fate in the shape of illness almost changed history in 1995 might want to consider that it cuts both ways. If Premier Bourassa had not been struck by cancer in the summer of 1990, he might have been less eager to clutch at the straws of the doomed Charlottetown Accord and more motivated to follow through on his proposal to put the question of sovereignty to Quebecers.

If he had, polls suggest he would have secured the kind of solid referendum mandate that neither federalists nor sovereignists believe is in the cards today. All of which is only to note—in closing—that in the dispensing of arbitrary acts of fate the gods of politics play for both sides.

IN LIEU OF AN INDEX

HÉBERT, LAPIERRE AND THE CAST

THE YES CAMP

Hébert: LUCIEN BOUCHARD first appeared on my reporting radar on March 31, 1988, when he stepped out of a chauffeured car at Rideau Hall to be sworn in to Prime Minister Brian Mulroney's cabinet. Until that morning he had been Canada's ambassador to France. His surprise appointment as secretary of state was the big news of the pre-election shuffle. He would turn out to be a gift to the media that would keep on giving, and the source of one of my few big scoops.

On an assignment for *Le Devoir* on Victoria Day 1990, I trekked up to Lucien Bouchard's Parliament Hill office—he had by then become the minister of the environment—to confirm a rumour that he was unhappy with the federal management of the constitutional file. The door to his office suite was closed but a window onto the hallway was open, presumably for air. Standing in the corridor, I quickly grew petrified as I overheard the minister's press secretary dictate Bouchard's letter of resignation from the cabinet and the Progressive Conservative caucus.

Le Devoir broke both the news of the resignation and published excerpts of the letter the next morning. For a long time the PMO believed I had extraordinary sources in Bouchard's entourage and vice versa. Good hearing is a key asset for a political journalist.

Lapierre: I worked (in vain) to stop LUCIEN BOUCHARD from entering the House of Commons when he first ran for a seat in Lac-Saint-Jean in 1988. For a Liberal MP from Quebec, as I was then, his arrival in the Tory ranks only months before a general election was bad news. Still, as an opposition critic, I enjoyed asking him questions in the House of Commons because he was long-winded and his answers would give us material to hold him to account. During the 1990 Meech Lake debacle I was stunned by his resignation from the government and his decision to turn against his good friend Brian Mulroney. When I too left my party in the wake of the simultaneous death of the Meech Lake Accord and Jean Chrétien's leadership victory, I approached Bouchard to see if we could form a rainbow coalition of independent MPs that would remain in Parliament long enough for Quebec to craft a new *rapport de forces* with the rest of Canada after the failure of Meech.

Creating a new Quebec-only party was initially not on our minds. Working with Bouchard on a daily basis, I came to appreciate his intelligence, his strong attachment to Quebec and even his political naivety. We became political partners. I kept the channels open with the provincial Liberal Party that was then in power in Quebec and he was close to the PQ. I left politics in 1992 and covered the 1995 referendum as a still-green political pundit, and it is from that purview that I saw how his pride and his indignation resonated with Quebecers. Our relationship became more delicate after he became premier and I had occasion to go hard on some of his government's policies. Our friendship has survived the years of professional distance and endures to this day.

Hébert: From eavesdropping at a federal minister's door, I moved on to eavesdropping at a dinner party. With his party leading in the provincial polls and on the heels of three by-election victories, Action Démocratique leader MARIO DUMONT was the main political attraction of a lobster dinner I attended in June 2002. For the better part of an hour I watched him hold court as some of the other diners pressed him for his views on a whole range of subjects and occasionally offered their help (and money) to get his party elected to power. They clearly wanted to be on the good side of a politician who seemed to be on the way up. As a real-life illustration of the unhealthy attraction that political power exerts on those who live off government procurement contracts, the scene was pretty graphic.

The dinner's guest list was ecumenical. It included municipal, provincial and federal politicians of all political stripes as well as some business leaders and a handful of journalists. For most of the evening, Jean Charest—then the leader of the Liberal opposition in the National Assembly—sat quietly with his wife at the other end of the head table. He did not have to fend off any admirers that night. But things were completely different a year later. By then Charest had been elected premier while Dumont had had to make do with a distant third place in the National Assembly and it was the former's flesh that everyone was seeking to press.

My next direct encounter with Dumont was less convivial. We happened to be together on the set of Radio-Canada's popular talk show *Tout le monde en parle* toward the end of the 2007 Quebec election campaign. The ADQ leader was there to talk up his party. I was there to promote my book on Stephen Harper and Quebec.

At that point in the campaign Dumont was on a roll and he was asked by the host to cost his platform, or at least his main promises. He could not or did not want to. When I was asked how I would rate his campaign, I questioned whether a leader who could not put a price on his policies this late in the campaign was ready for prime time. The heated exchange that followed apparently made for great television, if not a subtle approach to a politician I had to occasionally cover. The ADQ finished a close second to the Liberals in that election. In the years that followed, Dumont and his party indeed did not come across as ready for prime time as the official opposition role, and certainly not as a government-in-waiting.

Lapierre: I met **MARIO DUMONT** when he was the baby-faced president of the Quebec Young Liberals. A smart kid who loved to talk politics, he was then almost too mature for his age. We dined and golfed together while talking about the game of politics. In those early days, he came across as more of a true Liberal than the right-wing politician he would grow up to become.

When he broke ranks with Robert Bourassa's Liberals on a matter of principle, I admired his guts and his poise under pressure. It took some backbone to become leader of a new party and lead a campaign at such an early age. He ended his political career abruptly. Although I could easily see him moving on to Parliament Hill, he was never interested in federal politics. He would have been a great pick for Stephen Harper. We now both work together for the same TV network. I still believe he has a future in politics and that public life has not heard the last of him.

Hébert: I did not know **JACQUES PARIZEAU** except from the distance of Ottawa and Toronto in July 1995, when I broke the story of his "lobster trap" comment to some European Union ambassadors. The scoop came via a brown envelope. The federal officials who oversaw the planning of Canada's referendum response planted it. It nevertheless was a legitimate story that one of the ambassadors confirmed on the record before it went to print. But as I found out in the years after he left politics, Jacques Parizeau was always more than just a lifelong sovereignty warrior.

A few years later I moderated a policy discussion for the Canadian Association of Broadcasters in Vancouver. Preston Manning and Jacques Parizeau were both on the panel. One of its many highlights—at least from my perspective—was how they both agreed that their generation of leaders had done a poor job of managing the health care debate and allowed it to be smothered by partisan rhetoric. It was a fascinating afternoon that featured two very different politicians, each with the mind and the depth of true policy wonks. For similar reasons the two hours we spent at Parizeau's home as part of the research for this book were equally memorable.

Lapierre: My very first encounter with JACQUES PARIZEAU was remarkably cordial. As federal minister of youth and amateur sport in 1984 I had inherited the Loto-Canada file. Prime Minister John Turner wanted the money-losing federal lottery disbanded. I met Parizeau, who was then the Quebec minister of finance, at his farm in Foster to sound him out on the possibility that Ottawa devolve the jurisdiction for lotteries and casinos to the provinces. He could not have been more receptive.

A decade later I grew to dislike Parizeau for being a hard-core separatist, for his infamous speech on the night of the 1995 referendum and for perpetually meddling in the day-to-day life of the sovereignty movement. But I could never dispute his competency in fiscal and economic matters. It's only when we did the interview for this book that I came to appreciate the sincerity of his commitment to his cause and the clarity of his plan to take Quebec out of Canada.

Hébert: Until we went to his home in Verchères, my most recent encounter with BERNARD LANDRY dated back to the week before the 1995 referendum. We had sat in the same row of seats as we waited to go on (separately) a Télé-Québec current affairs program. As he watched Charles Taylor, Quebec's best-known philosopher, talk about the sorrow he would feel if the imminent referendum resulted in a Yes vote, Landry turned to me and confided that he was thinking of asking this articulate English-speaking federalist to head one of the new embassies of a sovereign Quebec. It was a rare insight into how certain the Yes camp was that victory was in sight.

Lapierre: BERNARD LANDRY has been a feature of the political scene for as long as I can remember. I did some shadowboxing with him when we formed the Bloc Québécois. He wanted it to be a branch plant of the Parti Québécois. I fought for it to remain an independent rainbow coalition. He finally won that battle after I left politics. Well versed in economics, he has been at the forefront of the transformation of the Quebec economy. A militant to this day, he clearly still regrets having resigned as leader of the PQ.

THE NO CAMP

Hébert: I covered LUCIENNE ROBILLARD for the first time during the campaign that cost her the provincial riding of Chambly in the 1994 Quebec election. In those days female star candidates were still very much the exception, and even more rare was the fact that in Chambly both the Liberals and the Parti Québécois were running strong women. If the PQ's Louise Beaudoin won the election, she was headed for a cabinet role. On the day I went to the riding, PQ leader Jacques Parizeau dropped in to give her a hand and Liberal leader Daniel Johnson was doing likewise for Robillard. Despite the high profile of these star candidates, both leaders struck me as quite comfortable treating them like props for their respective stump speeches.

The next time I saw Robillard in action, she had just been appointed as the federal minister in charge of liaising with the Quebec Liberals in the lead-up to the referendum. In that capacity she was attending her first meeting of the Quebec wing of the federal Liberal Party. When it comes to federalist fervor, more than six degrees separate the Quebec Liberals and their federal cousins. It was obvious that Robillard was not family to many in the room and that they did not know what to make of a Quebec nationalist acting as their representative on the No committee.

At her request, Robillard and I talked off the record in her Parliament Hill office for about an hour after the referendum. It must have been around the time when she realized the changes she had anticipated in the Quebec/Canada political relationship would not materialize. Her interview for this book reflects the unease that she had expressed at the time.

Lapierre: On radio I was never kind to LUCIENNE ROBILLARD. I routinely called her the archduchess of Westmount (her federal seat). She was not a media-friendly person and her shyness could make her appear haughty. To my shame, when I joined Paul Martin's cabinet in 2004, I discovered in Madame Robillard a competent, hard-working and honest person. And while she did not flaunt it, she was one of the most meticulous ministers at the table. To this day, I often use her as a sounding board before taking a delicate public position on an issue. Her judgment is solid and fact based. That approach is not necessarily an asset in partisan politics and it probably worked against her in the referendum saga.

Hébert: I first met JEAN CHAREST when he was the federal minister responsible for amateur sports in the summer of 1989. He was in Morocco for Les Jeux de la Francophonie. I was covering the two-week event for Radio-Canada. Neither of us knew that we were coming up to the end of our current roads. A month later, I left Radio-Canada for *Le Devoir* and Charest had to resign from Mulroney's cabinet the following winter for having called a judge on behalf of a constituent. We crossed paths again the following spring when he toured the country as the president of a parliamentary committee mandated to find enough chicken wire to hold the Meech Lake package together for a few months until it could be ratified by all the premiers.

Over the years I have made many trips to Sherbrooke— home to Jean Charest's federal and provincial ridings—as he launched his various election and leadership campaigns. Over that period he became my regular guest at the annual Parliamentary Press Gallery dinner. As a result I ended up taking a Tory minister, the Liberal leader of the opposition in the National Assembly and the Quebec premier to the dinner in relatively quick succession.

Lapierre: I met JEAN CHAREST on the hustings in 1984. I was a young MP for Shefford and he was the Tory candidate in the neighbouring riding of Sherbrooke. For years we engaged in a political cockfight for dominance of Quebec's Eastern Townships. In 1998, I called for and forced his resignation as minister of sports. I had become a pundit by the time he switched to provincial politics and, in that capacity, I questioned his liberal credentials and was underwhelmed by his first campaign as Quebec Liberal leader.

The dynamics between us changed dramatically when I became Quebec lieutenant for Prime Minister Paul Martin in 2004. Jean Charest was the premier and it was my responsibility to work with him and deliver political results for our province. We developed a very good working relationship and in hindsight our meetings were among the highlights of my brief mandate.

Hébert: I did not bring Jean Charest to one particular Gallery dinner, and it was one at which I got to rub elbows with DANIEL JOHNSON. On the first dinner after the referendum I invited Stéphane Dion instead. He had just left academia to become federal minister of intergovernmental affairs and take charge of the unity file. The Press Gallery tries to place guests with similar interests (and the same level of fluency in French) at the same table and Dion and Johnson ended up across from each other. But it was soon obvious that they were not of the same mind on the Quebec/Canada issue and that they had little to say to each other.

Before that dinner I had covered Johnson's first and only

election campaign as party leader in 1994, as well as his leadership of the referendum No campaign. On both occasions I had sat in on his meeting with *La Presse*'s editorial board. I had also co-interviewed him on a Sunday morning current affairs program. I clearly failed to make an impression.

The first time I went on *Tout le monde en parle* I was asked to name the leader I had found to be the least fun to cover. The question was as inane as it was unexpected and the only name that sprang to mind was Johnson's. It helped that he was retired from politics, so I would not have to cover him again. Alas, he still ate in Montreal restaurants and shortly after that broadcast he walked up to my table to suggest that my answer had no basis in fact since he did not recall that I had covered or interviewed him . . .

Lapierre: DANIEL JOHNSON has always been a mystery to me. I could never figure out how he could like politics and at the same time be so cold and distant with voters. His entourage kept telling us that he was so funny in private but I never saw much evidence of his much-praised sense of humour. As a minister and a premier he always had his ducks in a row. But as the referendum campaign confirmed, he could never deliver a barn-burning speech.

THE FEDS

Hébert: I was a Queen's Park correspondent when SHEILA COPPS first appeared in provincial politics. As in the House of

Commons a few years later, her arrival in the then-sedate Ontario Legislature generated quite a stir. In the early eighties women in Ontario politics were few and far between, and none was quite as combative and as outspoken as the new MPP for Hamilton Centre. At the time, the fact that she was both of those things in both official languages was even more remarkable.

In 1984, Copps switched to the federal scene, running for John Turner's Liberals. By then she already had one leadership campaign—against David Peterson—under her belt. Had she not made the move to the House of Commons, she would have become one of the youngest provincial ministers in the country. A year after she left Queen's Park for Parliament Hill, the Liberals took power in Ontario. By going to Ottawa, Copps had bought a ticket for a longer crossing of the opposition desert. As an MP she would have to wait another eight years before finally getting a taste of government. The second of her three leadership bids—against Jean Chrétien—took place over those federal opposition years.

I was in Hamilton on the night in 2004 when Copps was driven out of her riding and out of politics by fellow Liberal Tony Valeri, a Paul Martin loyalist. I thought at the time that her defeat was Martin's loss and that a party that engineered the fall of its icons was one that had lost its political compass.

Lapierre: I first encountered SHEILA COPPS when she was elected in 1984 and joined the Liberal caucus in Ottawa. She arrived with a knife between her teeth and went after Brian

Mulroney's jugular at every question period. That put us very much on the same page. With other Liberal colleagues we formed the "rat pack" and we made a bit of a name for ourselves as the party's attack team. Over that period I became known by the media as the "king of the clip," and with Sheila leading the pack we sometimes went overboard. I appreciated the fact that her heart was always in the right place on Quebec issues, bilingualism and the Constitution. She always stuck to her guns come hell or high water.

Hébert: At the last first ministers conference before the demise of the Meech Lake Accord in June 1990, **BRIAN TOBIN** and I chatted about the prospects for Newfoundland signing the deal in time for the late June ratification deadline. He confidently predicted that it would, and I suspect he had based that positive assessment on his own capacity to lobby Liberal members of the Newfoundland legislature in favour of the accord. But in the end Premier Clyde Wells did not put the accord to a vote, a decision that hammered the last nail in the Meech coffin.

When Tobin returned to Parliament Hill and the federal cabinet after having served only a few years as Newfoundland premier I wondered how someone who had become accustomed to being in control of a government would take to once again acting on the instructions of a prime minister (and his minions in the PMO). Indeed, his return to Ottawa was the first act of a bid to succeed Jean Chrétien, a move that I thought was problematic for another reason. Tobin did not have a good ear for French, a trait he shares with

Preston Manning. When he ultimately did not run for the leadership, I thought he had been wise to avoid getting crushed by Paul Martin's steamroller.

Lapierre: I was already an MP when BRIAN TOBIN was elected to the House of Commons in 1980. I was happy to have a young and energetic colleague who was a tenacious debater in the Newfoundland tradition. We both supported John Turner for leader in 1984, using our credentials as Young Turks to go aggressively after the "old backroom Liberals." Then our sharp tongues were put to good use against the Mulroney government as members of the "rat pack."

Hébert: The Liberal leadership match that PAUL MARTIN lost to Jean Chrétien in 1990 took place against the backdrop of the Meech Lake debate. Martin was pro-Meech; Chrétien was not. Many Quebec-based correspondents were sympathetic to Martin on the basis of his constitutional views. Notwithstanding Martin's Quebec-friendly approach, or perhaps because of it, I felt that he was momentum challenged. I reported that Chrétien—who was a less polished social animal but a more experienced politician—was also outperforming him in the debates. That assessment put me at odds with Martin's leadership team. It was then co-chaired by Jean Lapierre. It seems Martin and his crew got over it. A bit more than a decade later, as he was about to finally become prime minister, Martin offered me a senior communications role in the PMO. Since diplomacy is not my strongest suit, he is lucky that I declined.

Lapierre: My relationship with **PAUL MARTIN** predates his arrival in politics. When he was a prosperous businessman in Montreal he would call on me regularly to get my take on the pulse of Quebecers. I always admired his social conscience and his sensitivity to Quebec's aspirations. It was only natural for me to support him in his leadership bid of 1990. I was national co-chair of his leadership campaign with Iona Campagnolo. We stayed in contact after I left politics in 1992 and I once told him that if he ever became prime minister I would return to Parliament to give him a hand. That happened in 2004, when I left my media gig to run in Outremont, and become minister of transport and Martin's Quebec lieutenant. I still have a lot of time for him and admire his commitment to the causes he believes in.

Hébert: A few months before the referendum, **RAYMOND CHRÉTIEN** gathered the many diplomats who toil for Canada in the United States for a retreat that was held at the Pearson building, the Ottawa home of the foreign affairs department. I was invited to take part in a media panel that dealt with the domestic political climate.

At the time my perspective on the upcoming vote was greatly at odds with the climate of optimism that prevailed in the federal capital, and after I had concluded my remarks Chrétien took issue with my negative assessment of the federalist prospects. I in turn questioned whether approaching the referendum campaign as if voting against sovereignty was simply a no-brainer would get the federalist camp very far with Quebec voters. I think we both went home troubled after that exchange. I know that he subsequently discussed my remarks with the PMO.

Lapierre: I met RAYMOND CHRÉTIEN in the early 1980s when he was a civil servant and I was parliamentary secretary to the secretary of state for external affairs. I was impressed by his no-nonsense approach, his wit and his easy-going manner in a world of serious diplomats. His postings as ambassador placed him at the forefront of Canadian diplomacy and he clearly belonged there.

Hébert: I encountered ANDRÉ OUELLET's caricature some time before I met the actual person. When I took in a few Mulroney campaign speeches during the 1984 federal election, Ouellet was the Liberal's Quebec bogeyman, haunting the Tory campaign. In person he did not quite live up to the take-no-prisoner partisan character that Mulroney had made him out to be. But then maybe opposition had mellowed Ouellet. By the time I covered him in the late eighties, he was spending more time defending the Meech Lake Accord from some of his fellow Liberals than hunting down separatists. And when he decided to go public with the advice that Jean Charest should replace Daniel Johnson as leader of the Quebec Liberals after the referendum, I was the recipient of the end-of-year interview that started that particular ball rolling.

Lapierre: ANDRÉ OUELLET is my political mentor. He recruited me when I was still in college in Granby. I was already a young Liberal. I became his special assistant at the tender age of eighteen. He was then minister of consumer and corporate affairs. Two years later he moved on to urban affairs and took me along as his chief of staff. He encouraged me to take up law at the University of Ottawa and supported me in my every election campaign in Shefford. He taught me to respect people who run for elected office and to equate a political calling with public service.

Hébert: PRESTON MANNING showed up in my office at *Le Devoir* for an interview in his early days as Reform Party founder. I was surprised (and impressed) that he would bother with a newspaper that was as unlikely to be friendly to his cause as mine. He—as it turns out—was equally surprised that I would be interested in a Western Canada–based party such as his. In fact, a journalist trained to cover federalists and sovereignists on an equal footing, as those of us who cover the Quebec debate first-hand usually are, could only be professionally intrigued by a party such as Reform.

In 2000 I covered Manning's bid for the leadership of the Canadian Alliance—the party he had morphed the Reform into with the hope of expanding its base nationally. One weekend I tagged along with him on a tour of eastern Ontario. I remember that early Reform supporters would ask me once Manning had left their homes and gardens how his French measured up. I would have lied if I had said that it was good enough to campaign in Quebec. That was my first inkling that—taking Manning to his word that the party needed to grow roots in Central Canada—many Reformers were thinking of turning to the more bilingual Stockwell Day to lead them.

Lapierre: The first time I sat across from PRESTON MANNING was in the summer of 1990 on the "gold" floor of the Queen Elizabeth hotel in Montreal. I was with Lucien Bouchard and Manning was with Stephen Harper. Bouchard and I were in the process of forming the Bloc Québécois and the Reform Party was working its way onto the national radar. We had a frank exchange of views on what we hoped to accomplish in Ottawa. His view of Quebec's choices and their potential consequences was already crystal clear.

THE PREMIERS

Hébert: I can't think of ROY ROMANOW without thinking of Jean Chrétien. That's because I first caught a glimpse of the Saskatchewan politician at the 1981 first ministers meeting that concluded with the accord to bring the Constitution from Westminster to Canada. I was a junior Queen's Park correspondent; he was not yet a premier.

By the mid-nineties Romanow had moved from being Chrétien's behind-the-scenes ministerial pal in the constitutional talks to becoming the prime minister's staunchest ally at the federal-provincial table and, later, his appointee to head a royal commission into medicare. Until I started researching material for this book I did not know that Romanow had explored a contingency path for Saskatchewan separate from that of Chrétien's federal government for the event of a Yes vote. Apparently, the former Liberal prime minister did not know either.

When the premiers gathered in Ottawa to put the final touches to the Meech Lake Accord in late spring 1987, New Brunswick premier Richard Hatfield found himself at the centre of a traffic-stopping scrum. As he tried to walk his way up from the Château Laurier hotel to the Langevin Block and Brian Mulroney's office on Wellington Street, Hatfield was engulfed in a sea of cameras and microphones. Everyone wanted to know if he would pass the Meech Lake Accord in the New Brunswick legislature before calling an election.

He did not and soon lost all the province's seats to FRANK MCKENNA's Liberal Party. McKenna had also objected to the accord, as it was then drafted—the unravelling of the Meech deal started with his election victory. By June 1990 the premier had come around to supporting the accord, but his initial doubt was the first of the thousand cuts that eventually killed the deal. I know that he meant his early criticism to be constructive. I'm not sure he would go the same route, knowing all that he knows today.

I first ran across MIKE HARRIS in 1981 on a campaign whistle stop in North Bay. Progressive Conservative premier Bill Davis was campaigning hard to end a six-year minority spell. Harris was running in a Liberal-held seat that Tory strategists had identified as winnable.

By that point in the late-winter campaign, journalists on the tour could recite the premier's stump speech in their sleep, and candidates on the occasion of such visits are mostly expected to smile and look happy. As a result it was not Harris who initially made a strong impression on the jaded press corps but rather the quality of the homemade cakes his volunteers had prepared for the media.

Many of those volunteers were French-speaking, a rarity on the Tory campaign trail, as Davis's party was not considered as friendly to French-language rights as the Liberals or the NDP. For once, over my time on the Davis campaign, I got to run some clips in French in my report. On March 19, 1981, the riding of Nipissing did hand Harris his ticket to the Ontario legislature.

I had moved on to Parliament Hill by the time he became Ontario's Progressive Conservative premier almost fifteen years later, and I followed his tenure in power only from the relative distance of federal-provincial deliberations. At first ministers meetings his politically incorrect friendship with Lucien Bouchard certainly stood out. Together the two premiers took on Jean Chrétien on a variety of issues including health care funding. We had never spoken face to face until he agreed to sit down for the interview in this book.

Until **BOB RAE** launched a bid to become the leader of the Ontario NDP, I knew of him only as the up-and-coming Member of Parliament who had moved the 1979 non-confidence motion that ended Tory prime minister Joe Clark's brief sojourn in power and ushered Pierre Trudeau's Liberals back to office in February 1980.

As a Queen's Park correspondent with Radio-Canada, I spent a lot of my time on the lookout for MPPs who could provide thirty-second clips in French. On that score Rae, who with Jean Charest is one of the most fluently bilingual leaders I have covered, was a providential addition to the Ontario lineup. For a short period at the time of the 1985 provincial election, Ontario's three main leaders—Tory Frank Miller, Liberal David Peterson and Bob Rae—were all bilingual enough to give interviews in French. There were times when that led to some frustration in the Queen's Park press gallery, as some of the unilingual correspondents rightly feared that they might miss out on some news.

I spent the last week of the 1990 Ontario election campaign on the road with the various provincial leaders and got to watch first hand as Bob Rae was transformed from third-party leader going through the motions of what had widely been expected to be a losing campaign, to unexpected winner of the election by the magic wand of the electorate. When he set out a few years later to recast himself as a federal Liberal leader and an aspirant for the post of prime minister, it seemed to me that anyone who had unexpectedly risen out of the opposition ashes to become a phoenix at Queen's Park, as he had in September 1990, would have a quasi-unshakable faith in the capacity of voters to breathe new life into a politician.

Lapierre: I never had much time for **BOB RAE** when he was an NDP member in Ottawa. He really appeared on my radar— as he did for many other Canadians—when he became premier of Ontario. I was not terribly impressed. But there was no denying his depth, his energy and his natural oratory talent, and all of those were in evidence when he ran for the federal Liberal leadership in 2006. Although I thought that his record as premier of Ontario would be an impediment for a federal victory, he would have made an interesting leader for my former party.

THE LAST WORD

Lapierre: I have known JEAN CHRÉTIEN since 1974 when I was a young ministerial assistant in Ottawa. I always saw him as a "jolly good fellow," an influential minister and a down-to-earth politician, but I could never convince myself that he had the depth and the royal jelly to become prime minister. That explains why I supported John Turner in 1984 and Paul Martin in 1990. The people of Canada have proven me wrong at every electoral turn.

We worked together in the 1980 referendum and on the patriation of the Constitution in 1982, and our relationship only really soured in the lead-up to the failure of the Meech Lake Accord. With tensions running high, I once called him "Quebec's Uncle Tom," an unwarranted statement that was way out of line. Nonetheless, at the time of the 1995 referendum, I did believe that he was out of touch with Quebecers—including fellow federalists. His negligence almost led to the breaking up of the federation.

Hébert: In the spring of 1984 Radio-Canada sent me to the University of Western Ontario to take a short course in law and journalism. But I skipped out to go to Ottawa so I could watch the Liberal leadership convention that would name Pierre Trudeau's successor. The election of John Turner over JEAN CHRÉTIEN was a triumph of the party elites over the grassroots members. Without the locked-in support of much of the Liberal establishment for Turner, the outcome and perhaps history would have been different. I have yet to cover any prime minister for as long as I covered Jean Chrétien. Perhaps I never will.

REFERENDUM POSTCARDS FROM

JUSTIN TRUDEAU

Justin Trudeau watched at home with his father and a few friends from McGill University as the results came in from the 1995 referendum. In Pierre Trudeau's house there was only one television set. "My father was very stoic throughout the evening. He did not say much. But when it was over and one of my friends noted that it had been a close vote, he said: the No has won."

Of the men who now lead Canada's main federalist parties, the Liberal leader was the furthest removed from the action in 1995. He had just returned from a backpacking world tour. He was a student at McGill. He was not at all political in the partisan sense of the word. "I participated in the referendum as an interested citizen," he says.

In that capacity, Trudeau attended the pro-Canada rally. He feels it was a seminal event whose impact outlasted the referendum campaign itself. "I don't know if it was a good or bad tactical move but it was an opportunity for Canadians to express their attachment to Quebec and that was important."

He did vote on referendum day but he is unsure that his ballot made it into the count. "I pressed really hard on the pencil to mark my ballot and it may have been thrown out." He says that does not faze him as he figures that if his vote and others like his were not counted, the margin of victory for the No actually might have been higher than the total reported. In any event he was happy to be in Montreal for referendum night. "I had missed the first one. I was only nine years old at the time and I lived in Ottawa."

His father, Pierre, was the big federalist star of the 1980 referendum, but he was completely absent from the 1995 campaign stage. There are those who feel it was wrong to keep the former prime minister out of the federalist lineup. Justin Trudeau is not one of them. "It was not his referendum. He was out of public life. Another genera-tion was in charge."

The Liberal leader did draw two lessons from the expe-rience. The first is common to most federalists who fought for the No side in 1995 and it pertains to the need for a clearer question. "I knew lots of people who were voting yes because they wanted a better deal for Quebec in Canada. A complicated question resulted in an outcome that did not accurately reflect actual support for sovereignty."

The second is less referendum, or Quebec, specific: there is a significant gap between the tactical messaging that consumes politicians and their handlers and what actu-ally resonates with ordinary voters. While strategists are consumed by details, it is the broad strokes that matter to voters. "It's important for me to remember, as I now live in an environment dominated by strategy and tactics, that, back in 1995, even I—someone who was keenly interested in the referendum—did not really follow who was saying what or who had given which referendum speech where."

THOMAS MULCAIR

Thomas Mulcair spent the day of the 1995 referendum ferrying voters to his riding's polling stations. It was the future federal NDP leader's second referendum campaign but his first as an elected MNA. He had won the provincial seat of Chomedey under the Quebec Liberal banner a year earlier. What he remembers most about that day is the fear of some constituents that their ballots would go uncounted on a series of technicalities. "We had a lot of volunteers and many were experienced. Women who lived and breathed politics would come back from voting in tears because they had been told that if their cross were not completely within the box, it would be declared invalid." The issue of deliberately wasted federalist ballots was one he pursued after the referendum.

Like Justin Trudeau, Mulcair attended the pro-Canada rally. He felt it helped the federalist cause. He has a lot less praise for Jean Chrétien's performance in the last week of the campaign. "For the entire referendum campaign we [the Quebec Liberals] had waited for some gesture from Ottawa and none came until the day when shaking, white as a sheet and looking ten years older than his age, Chrétien finally blubbered some opaque commitment."

Mulcair describes the prime minister's eleventh-hour conversion to the distinct society cause "a mea culpa delivered by body language that may have helped by convincing some voters that they had at least succeeded in making Jean Chrétien nervous."

Mulcair says he encountered the so-called Bouchard effect on the doorsteps of his riding. He remembers how one constituent in particular told him that she had voted for him in the Quebec election and would do so again in the next one but that she had to vote yes "because Monsieur Bouchard had suffered so much for Quebecers."

The NDP leader does not believe that if there ever is another referendum it will be based on a question as convoluted as the 1995 one; but he feels that raising the threshold for a future sovereignty mandate is a mug's game. He calls it a way for the rest of Canada to hide itself behind a "protective veil" rather than address some of the core irritants in the Quebec/Canada relationship.

From Mulcair's perspective, a lack of reciprocal respect—"the notion that we could insult each other and hurt each other at will"—contributed mightily to the 1995 showdown. "I would argue that we no longer insult each other as gratuitously as we used to," he suggests, thinking back to the constitutional crisis of the early nineties and the hot language elicited in some quarters. One can always hope that he is right!

ACKNOWLEDGEMENTS

A n army of guardian angels of various political persuasions hovered over the contents of this book.

Their comments were generally not for attribution and they shall remain anonymous.

But their insights added invaluable texture to the story. Twenty years later it appears that they all still like the politicians they served under in 1995.

Steven Hogue and Lisette Lapointe made the indispensable Chrétien and Parizeau interviews happen. One can only hope that when they read the book the former prime minister and premier will not curse them for having interceded in our favour.

Knopf Canada senior editor Craig Pyette enticed me to think about writing a second book. He then earned my forgiveness and my gratitude by putting hours into making the text more fluid.

This book is dedicated to Jean's three and my two grandchildren. They will have to grow up some more before they read it, as it lacks a happy ending.

Chantal Hébert is a national affairs writer with the *Toronto Star* and a guest columnist for *L'Actualité*. She is a weekly participant on the political panel "At Issue" on CBC's *The National* as well as Radio-Canada's *Les Coulisses du pouvoir*. Her first book was *French Kiss: Stephen Harper's Blind Date with Quebec*. Hébert is a past recipient of the Hyman Solomon Award for Excellence in Public Policy Journalism.

Jean Lapierre is a political commentator for CTV and TVA television networks. He has a daily commentary on the Cogeco radio stations and on CJAD Montreal. In his previous life as a Member of Parliament he served in John Turner's and Paul Martin's Liberal cabinets. In between he was a founding member of the Bloc Québécois.